HEAL THYSELF
Natural Living
COOKBOOK

A Complete Guide to
Natural Living
through
Vegetarian Cooking
and Holistic Juicing

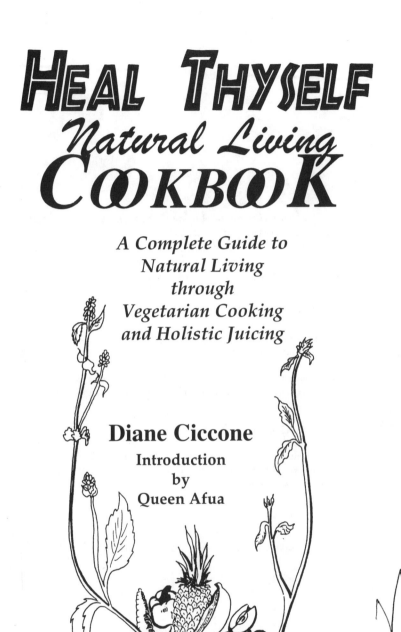

Diane Ciccone

Introduction
by
Queen Afua

A&B PUBLISHERS GI
Brooklyn, New Yo
11238

D0711554

COVER CONCEPT: *A & B PUBLISHERS GROUP*
ILLUSTRATION: *MSHINDO I.*

The Publisher wishes to thank the *Heal Thyself Organization* and *Natural
Planetary Healers* for reproduction of selected material and Shirley McRae.

ISBN: 1-886433-05-4

The contents of this book are merely for the purpose of education and
information . This book is not intended to serve as a substitute for
medical supervision.

Manufactured in Canada

No Meat No Eggs No Salt

Table of Contents

Introduction..1
Foreword...3
Acknowledgement 5
Preparing Your Kitchen 7
Section 1: Breakfast 11
Section 2: Appetizers...18
Section 3: Beverages 25
Section 4: Live Juices...37
Section 5: Salads/Dressings 45
Section 6: Soups/Stews..63
Section 7: Marinade/Sauces & Dips.....................71
Section 8: Main Dishes 79
     vegetables......................................81
     grain-based 94
     noodles 97
     tofu/tempeh 101
Section 9: Children Menus.............................105
Section 10: Desserts..111
     cookies 113
     cakes and frostings 116
     fruits 119
     pies/tarts......................................122
Section 11: Herbal "Folk" Recipes.........................129
Section 12: Charts 141
Index: 154

Introduction

IN THESE CHALLENGING TIMES ON EARTH, RAMPANT dis-ease, and suffering are occurring because of the many poor choices that we have made. But we can rest assured that there is a way out. If we make productive choices we all can experience health and wholeness in our lives. The creator is always present and always supportive in our need to be well in Body, Mind and Soul. The Most High never fails to send us guides to aid us on our return to our natural birthright, *to be well.*

One of such guides is Diane Ciccone. Through her divine love and work with holistic foods and juices by way of the *"Heal Thyself Natural Living Cookbook"* we are given the opportunity to Heal Thyself.

So much present day anger, stress and premature aging is derived from our constant daily intake of fast foods, man-made process foods and devitalized foods. On the other hand consuming natural foods of fresh fruits, vegetables, whole grains, seeds, nuts and live juices, along with specific herbs and spices, enable us to experience joy, peace, harmony, longevity, vitality and a body free of dis-ease. For you see, *"we truly are what we eat."*

Once you learn how to prepare God's foods naturally, with these wonderful wholesome recipes created and compiled by Diane, you will observe how beautiful your life unfolds. The recipes contained within these pages are a traditional diet of fuller heavier meatless meals to simpler uncooked vegetarian meals. Remember less is better! You will find that the lighter simpler foods give you greater power and strength which in the end help you to manifest a more masterful productive life.

1

Diane Ciccone's has been living on the "Heal Thyself Path of Purification," for over 26 years. She was among the first to graduate as a Certified Heal Thyself Professor of Purification, and wrote this work of natural living so that we could have a *Natural Living* Dietary Guide to live harmony with nature, ourselves, our families, our neighbors and the universe.

The foundation of this work stems from the Heal Thyself Principle that your kitchen is your laboratory. The most crucial room within your home for restoring and purifying the body temples is none other than that knowledge that is contained within your "Kitchen Laboratory." From internalization and incorporating these readings, you too will have the power to Heal Thyself.

QUEEN AFUA
Director *Heal Thyself Living Center*
Best-selling Author of *"Heal Thyself for Health and Longevity"*

Foreword

IHAVE BEEN VEGETARIAN FOR OVER TWENTY SIX YEARS. During that time the most frequently asked questions, were: "Isn't eating only vegetables boring?" and "I wouldn't know how to cook a vegetarian meal, how do you do it?" This book is designed to answer both questions and a little more.

The Heal Thyself Natural Living Center's philosophy is; *The key to good wholesome living is living a clean wholesome life. That begins with eating clean wholesome food.*

This cookbook is dedicated and written for those who want to cook and eat clean wholesome food. All recipes are animal, sugar and salt free. Many are also oil free.

Although a vegetarian diet with a high percentage of live food is ideal, many of us for whatever reason cannot or do not eat vegetarian recipes. If you are beginning on a vegetarian diet, many of the heavy "carbohydrate" recipes will make your transition from a meat based diet to a vegetable based diet easier. As you adjust to a vegetarian diet, you should use more of the live foods and juice recipes in your meal planning. If you have a high percentage of live food in your diet or are beyond a "sophomore level" in Queen Afua's Natural Living Program many of the "heavier" recipes which contain tofu, nuts, rice, gravies or pasta may be too heavy and should not be eaten. In many cases, the "heavier" vegetarian recipes can be adapted to reflect a lighter more *live* diet. This cookbook keeps this in mind. You will soon learn that a healthy wholesome diet can be exciting, creative and fun.

ENJOY!

Acknowledgment

I GIVE THANKS AND PRAISES TO THE CREATOR, WITHOUT whom none of this would have been possible.

I wish to thank Queen Afua for gently encouraging me to support this project.

I thank my family, Daryl and Kali, for their patience, support and inspiration.

Thanks to the Professors of Purification for their recipes and many other folks through the years.

Special thanks to Gloria for her beautiful illustrations.

Many thanks to Shirley McRae my editor and friend.

Diane Ciccone

Preparing Your Kitchen

MANY PEOPLE WHO ARE MAKING THE TRANSITION TO a natural living (vegetarian) diet are concerned about what they need in their kitchen. A well stocked natural living kitchen is not very different from any other kitchen. I have prepared a brief list of the type of items which are helpful in your preparation of a natural living meal.

Pots/Pans

Stainless steel or glass is preferable. Avoid Aluminum and Teflon. Medical studies have linked cooking in aluminum pots to Alzheimer's disease.

Utensils

A good set of knives is invaluable for cutting/slicing fruits and vegetables. Large wooden spoons are good for mixing. I prefer wood to plastic or metal spoons for mixing, however, they can be used.

A note about plastic: we should all be ecologically conscious and cut back on our plastic use.

Storage Containers

Large glass mason jars are an excellent way to store your grains, flours and pastas. A bay leaf in each jar will help keep grains and flours free from bugs.

A note about storing: unless you use your flours and oils in a short period of time, they are better kept in the refrigerator to prevent rancidity.

Food Processors

Although this is an optional item, some recipes that requires food to be chopped very fine are best prepared in a food processor. If you cook in large quantities, food processors can cut down on preparation time. As you begin to eat more live meals a food processor becomes invaluable.

Pressure Cooker/Crock Pot

This is optional. If your budget allows, go for it. The pressure cooker/crock pot cuts down on cooking times.

Blenders

This is used in many beverages recipes and is a must for every kitchen.

Steamers

There are electric, ceramic and metal steamers. Which steamer you choose depends on your budget. The least expensive is the metal steamer basket which is placed inside the cooking pot and covered.

Juicers

A must for anyone on a natural living diet.

FOOD STOCK

Spices

Powders are preferable to salts, *i.e.,* garlic, onion, celery powders. If needed, there are many salt substitutes on the market. Cayenne pepper is preferable to black pepper. Black pepper irritates the intestinal lining. Always buy non-irradiated spices. They will be labeled and are generally found in health food stores.

Sweeteners

Honey, maple syrup, molasses, barley malt and date sugar are excellent natural substitutes to sugar.

Condiments

I highly recommend a trip to your local health food store. You can substitute ALL your present condiments with ones that are sugar and salt free as well as free of animal products and by-products. The key to purchasing any product is to read the labels. Many products use the word "natural," but are still laden with sugar, salt and animal products or by-products.

Sprouts

Can be purchased in grocery or health food stores. However, the cheapest way is to grow your own. An excellent resource book is Ann Wigmore's, *The Sprouting Book.*

Some Items That You May Want To Keep On Hand

Liquid Lecithin & Granules	Flax Seeds
Egg Replacer	Psyllium Husks
Wheat Germ	Apple Cider Vinegar

Herbs

What you use depends on your own tastes. Herbs are a good source of seasoning as well as being good for you. Fresh herbs in your recipes give more flavor. Herbs are easy to grow, if you don't have a garden, plant in pots and put in a window.

Section 1

Breakfast

Breakfast

IN OUR HOUSE, SUNDAY BREAKFAST WAS A MEAL where no one was rushing to go anywhere and we could all eat together. My mother would fix pancakes, eggs, bacon, sausage or ham. Although the meal time was special, the heavy starch and grease of the pork would leave my stomach in distress for the rest of the day. Many years later, I realized the importance of that first meal, break-fast, for it is the meal that can set the tone for the entire day.

The following recipes are "heavy" vegetarian meals. They are ideal if you are in a transition diet or to eat that "special" and "rare occasion." not to be eaten more than once or twice a week. Those following the Natural Living Program should drink the pre-breakfast followed by a live juice or fresh fruit meal.

Pre Breakfast Drink

  1 lemon, juiced
  1 grapefruit, juiced
  1 orange, juiced
  8-16 ounces warm water

Mix all ingredients.

NOTE: Do not eat for at least ½ hour.

French Toast

Batter:

  1½ cups tofu
  1 teaspoon ground cinnamon
  2 tablespoons real maple syrup

  ½ cup water or soy milk

Bread:

  8 slices day-old whole grain bread

In a blender, blend all ingredients until smooth.

Pour into a shallow dish.

Dip the bread in the batter, then fry on a hot griddle or skillet in butter or oil until golden brown on both sides.

Alternative: Bake at 350° F on a well oiled pan until golden on each side.

Breakfast Rice Pudding

½ cup cooked brown rice

½ cup milk (soy)

½ teaspoon vanilla

1 tablespoon toasted wheat germ

2 tablespoons broken nuts or sunflower seeds

1 teaspoon molasses

cinnamon or nutmeg (optional)

Combine all ingredients in a small saucepan.
Gently cook, covered, for five minutes.
Serve warm, with a sprinkle of cinnamon or nutmeg, if desired.

Makes one serving

Scrambled Tofu

1 pound tofu, crumbled (squeeze out excess water)

1 small onion, chopped

1 small pepper, chopped

¼ teaspoon garlic powder

¼ teaspoon turmeric

1 teaspoon nutritional yeast

chopped chives to taste

Sauté onion and pepper in water.
Add tofu, mash with a fork until completely crumbled.
Add remaining ingredients, mix well all the flavors.
This is done over a low flame.

Muesil

4 ounces rolled oats

2 ounces figs, chopped

1 ounce hazelnuts, chopped

½ teaspoon ground cinnamon

2 apples, grate just before serving

Place oats and figs in a bowl, add water just to cover. Leave overnight in cover bowl.

Before serving add the remaining ingredients and mix well.

Serve with soy milk or any nut milk.

Crunchy Granola

Mix dry ingredients together:

4 cups rolled oats

½ cup coconut

¾ cup slightly roasted nut (peanut or other)

½ cup pumpkin or sunflower seeds

Mix in separate bowl and add to dry ingredients:

¾ tablespoon honey

1 tablespoon vanilla

¼ cup oil

Mix together thoroughly and spread on shallow edge baking sheet.

Bake at 300° F for 45 minutes until light brown.

Reduce heat to 225° F and bake until dry.

Stir occasionally while baking.

Add ½ cup raisins or chopped nuts.

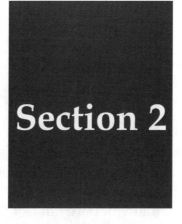

Section 2

Appetizers

Appetizers

How many of those social gatherings have you gone to and the appetizers that you could possibly choose from were: chips, nuts, raw broccoli and carrots with a dip that you dare not ask the contents? Well, here are few suggestions for the hostess.

Marinated Mushrooms

4 cups small fresh mushrooms (about 1 pound)
1 cup water
½ cup brown rice or apple cider vinegar
1 bay leaf
1 clove garlic, sliced or quartered
2 to 3 sprigs fresh basil (or pinch dried basil)
2 to 3 sprigs fresh thyme or oregano (or pinch dried thyme or oregano)
2 tablespoons olive oil, preferably Italian
2 tablespoons silvered scallion
1 tablespoon minced parsley
parsley sprigs and strips of fresh lemon peel for garnish

This appetizer requires only 10 minutes of preparation time. Let the mushrooms marinate at least 12 hours, but no longer than three days.

Wash mushrooms, trim stems, and place caps in a heat proof bowl. Set aside.

Combine water, vinegar, bay leaf, garlic and herbs in a small saucepan.

Bring mixture to a boil, simmer no more than 1 minute, add oil after removing from heat, and pour over mushrooms.

Allow to cool, then cover bowl and refrigerate at least 12 hours before serving. Toss occasionally so mushrooms will marinate evenly.

To serve, drain mushrooms and remove bay leaf, garlic and herb sprigs. Toss mushrooms and slivered scallion and minced parsley. Place in a serving bowl and garnish with parsley sprigs and lemon peel.

Makes 4 cups. Serves 32

Carrot Pate

Carrot Mixture:

      1 cup water

      2 cups chopped carrots

      ¼ teaspoon dill weed

      ½ teaspoon salt-free vegetable seasoning

      ½ teaspoon vegetable protein powder

      ¼ teaspoon granulated garlic

      2½ teaspoons nutritional yeast

      ¾ teaspoon granulated onion

Other:

      2 tablespoons unroasted sesame seed oil

      4 tablespoons finely-ground, whole wheat flour

Blend carrot mixture ingredients until smooth; pour into pot and simmer 10 minutes on top of stove.

Brown wheat flour in sesame oil, then add to hot carrot mixture to thicken.

Cool. Use as a spread, dip, or for canapés.

Note: The oil is the smoothing element, which also keeps the pate moist.

Cauliflower Couscous Pate

4 cups steamed, well-done cauliflower pieces

4 cups steamed couscous, prepared according to standard directions.

Blend above ingredients, still hot, in blender or food processor.

2 teaspoons granulated garlic

1½ teaspoons onion powder

½ teaspoons ground nutmeg

¼ teaspoons ground cayenne pepper

In a blender or food processor, combine all ingredients with the couscous mixture and until smooth.

Serve piping hot.

This recipe can also be used as an appetizer spread on canapés. or as a dip for crackers.

Yield: 6 cups

Stuffed Celery Sticks

1 mashed avocado, seasoned with lemon juice

⅛ teaspoon kelp
Celery stalks

Cut the celery in 5 inch lengths and fill with avocado.

Variations: Stuff celery with tofu eggless salad (pg.58); carrot, olive or cauliflower pate (pg. 20)

Stuffed Endive Leaves

8 ounces fresh tofu

¼ cup mellow white miso
2 tablespoons lemon juice or brown rice vinegar
2 tablespoons safflower or sesame oil
1 clove garlic, finely minced or pressed
3 tablespoons fresh minced onion (or 2 tablespoons dried onion)

½ cup minced red bell pepper

½ cup minced celery
20 Belgian endive leaves (separated from two to three large Belgian endive)
20 sprigs watercress

Place tofu in boiling water to cover.
Turn off heat, cover, let sit a few minutes, then place the tofu in cold water to cool.
Remove tofu, wrap in cheesecloth or porous cotton, and gently squeeze out excess water.

Place tofu, miso, juice or vinegar, oil and garlic in a blender and blend until smooth. Stir in onion, pepper and celery. Let rest, refrigerated, at least 2 hours to allow flavors to heighten. The stuffing mixture can be made one or two days in advance if kept covered in the refrigerator.

At serving time, taste tofu mixture and adjust seasonings. Place a heaping teaspoon of tofu mixture on the lower third of each endive leaf.

Tuck a sprig of watercress into the mixture so it rests on the endive leaf.

Place the pieces on a platter in a fan shape, or other attractive arrangement.

Makes 20 appetizers.

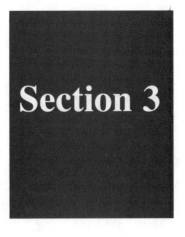

Section 3

Beverages

Beverages

With all the "artificial" beverages on the market *i.e.,* soda, fruit punch, koolades, etc.. I wanted to give some simple yet tasty alternatives. For those who can not live without milk, there are nut milks which are nutritious substitutes for cow's or goat's milk.

Enjoy, but remember drink fluids at least ½ an hour to 1 hour before or after your meal, but *NEVER* during your meal.

Rice Milk

4 cups water
1 cup brown rice, cooked
1 teaspoon vanilla (optional)

Blend ingredients in blender or food processor until smooth.
Refrigerate. Shake before using.

Nut & Seed Milk

½ cup almonds
½ cup sesame seeds or cashews
1 quart water
2 tablespoons maple syrup

Blend ingredients until smooth.

Coconut Milk

1½ cups fresh coconut, shredded or grated
1 quart water
2 tablespoons sunflower oil

Blend ingredients until smooth.

Note: use only raw nuts. All nuts should be soaked in water overnight.

Coconut-Almond Milk

½ cup coconuts
½ cup almonds
5 dates
1 quart water

Blend ingredients until smooth.

Banana Smoothie:

1 cup soy milk
1 cup ice
3 medium-size bananas
2 tablespoons honey

Blend ingredients until smooth.

Comfrey Pineapple Cooler

2 cups pineapple juice
1 cup fresh comfrey leaves
1 sprig fresh mint
Handful of fresh parsley or watercress

Orange juice can be substituted for the pineapple juice.
Combine all ingredients in a blender and process until
smooth.

Serves 2

Melon-Orange Frappe

2 cups fresh melon chunks
1 cup fresh orange juice
1 cup crushed ice

Blend all ingredients until smooth

Serves 2

Hot Spiced Cider

1 gallon apple cider
2 oranges
2 lemons
8 whole cloves
1 stick cinnamon
1 teaspoon whole allspice

Slice oranges and lemons, remove seeds.
Cut slices in half (leave on rind).
Put all ingredients in large pan;
Bring to boiling point, but do not boil.
Serve piping hot.

To reheat leftover cider, remove spices.

Fruit 'n' Flax

1 tablespoon flax seed meal
6 ounces fruit juice
1 small banana
1 ice cube

Blend flax seed and juice. Let stand 10 minutes.
Add banana and ice cube and blend until smooth.

Grape Spritzer

2½ cups chilled white grape juice
1½ cups chilled sparkling water
lime or lemon wedges
frozen green grapes
(optional garnish)

Choose elegant glasses.
Fill each with 5 ounces grape juice and 3 ounces sparkling water.
Add a small cluster of frozen green grapes and a slice of lime or lemon.

Serves 4

Mint Cooler

½ cup fresh mint leaves

½ cup natural lemonade

⅓ cup lime juice drink

4 or 6 ice cubes

1 slice of lime

Combine mint leaves, lemonade, lime juice drink and ice cubes in a blender and blend until smooth.
Twist the lime slice and place on top.
Serve immediately.

Orange Mist

1 cinnamon orange tea bag

⅓ cup boiling water

½ cup orange juice

4 to 6 ice cubes

¼ cup sparkling water

Pour boiling water over the tea bag and steep for 5 minutes.
Remove the tea bag.
Put the tea, juice and ice cubes into a blender and blend until smooth.
Add sparkling water and serve immediately.

Tea & Fruit Pop

½ cup prepared herbal tea
½ cup carbonated fruit juice, such as sparkling
tangerine juice
Brown rice malt syrup, to taste

In a tall glass or pitcher, combine the tea, several ice cubes and the fruit juice of your choice.

If desired, sweeten to taste with the brown rice syrup.

Apple Whiz

Add four bags of cinnamon tea to one quart unfiltered apple juice. Let sit for several hours.

Refrigerate, serve over ice.

Sun Tea Cocktails

6 bags herbal tea or equivalent loose tea
2 cups water
maple syrup to taste
2 cups ice cubes
2 cups chilled sparkling water

Prepare sun tea. Stir in maple syrup and add ice cubes. Stir until thoroughly chilled. Add sparkling water.

Serves 6

Ginger Ale

2 lemons
1 quart fresh water
1 cup fresh ginger root, peeled and chopped
1 quart sparkling water
honey
dash of cayenne pepper (optional)

Peel the lemons and cut the peels into thin strips.
Place in a saucepan with ginger.
Add four cups fresh water and bring to a boil.
Cover and let steep for 10 minutes.
Strain and add honey and juice of peeled lemon to taste.
A pinch of cayenne pepper adds zip. Chill.
To serve, add one part sparkling water to three parts ginger mix.
Add ice.

Makes about 2 quarts.

Serves 6 - 8

Tropical Fruit Tea

2 quarts water
3 tablespoons hibiscus flowers
3 tablespoons mint leaves
3 tablespoons lemon grass
½ cup pineapple, chopped
2 oranges, sliced
1 papaya, slice
1 mango or other tropical fruit (optional)

Bring water to a boil, turn off the heat and add the hibiscus, mint and lemon grass.
Let steep 20 minutes and strain.
Put the fruits into a 2 quart jar and pour the tea over them.
Refrigerate overnight.

Root Beer

½ cup each: cinnamon, sarsaparilla, sassafras, winter-green
1 quart water
½ cup honey
3 cups carbonated water

Simmer herbs in water for 10 minutes.
Strain out herbs.
Add honey and cool.
Add carbonated water before serving.

Hot Carob Drink

1½ cups soy milk
2 teaspoons carob powder
1 teaspoon honey
dash of vanilla extract

½ teaspoon cinnamon

Blend all ingredients and heat gently

Serves 1

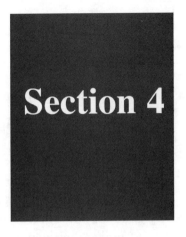

Section 4

"Live Juices"

Live Juices

"**L**IVE JUICES" ARE THE JUICE OF ANY FRESH FRUITS OR vegetables. By drinking "live juice" the body is able to assimilate and utilize the vitamins and minerals from the fruit or vegetable. This is beneficial whether you are healthy and using live juice as preventive maintenance or if you are on a program designed to help rid the body of dis-ease.

Live juices are essential to any fasting or natural living program . Live juice will provide you with the vitamins, minerals and amino acids needed to detoxify, build and repair your body. Please refer to Queen Afua's book, "*Heal Thyself with Health and Longevity*" for a complete discussion of the benefits of Juice Fasting.

A few "musts" when drinking live juice:

1. Thoroughly wash and scrub the skins to remove all dirt. Use Dr. Bronner's soap or commercial washes—available in health food stores—to remove pesticides and chemical residue For foods that have been waxed, cut off the skin before juicing. Whenever possible use organic fruits and vegetables.

2. Any live juice must be consumed within 15 minutes. Virtually all the minerals and vitamins are lost through oxidation after 15 minutes.

3. Fruit juice will detoxify and cleanse the body of accumulated waste. Vegetable juice will build and repair the body.

The following recipes are only a sample of the countless variations. Be creative!

VEGETABLE JUICE COMBINATIONS

Carrot Ginger Zing

5 carrots, cleaned and cut to fit in juicer

½" root of fresh ginger

Note: The "zing" can be modified by the amount of ginger used.

Veggie Cocktail

3 carrots
3 celery stalks

Wash and juice all ingredients.

Spring Sweep

5 carrots
1 beet

Wash and juice all ingredients.

Cucumber Cooler

2 cucumbers, peeled
1 carrot

Wash and juice all ingredients.

Blood Sugar Tonic*

    1 cup alfalfa sprouts
    1 cup mung sprouts
    1 cup lentil sprouts
    2 kale leaves
    1 cup Jerusalem artichokes
    1 handful string beans
    1 medium parsnip
    ½ cup fennel

Wash ingredients. Combine, juice and serve.

*Submitted by Ada Robinson, Professor of Purification and Assistant to Queen Afua.

Carrot & Turnip

    5 carrots
    1 turnip

Wash and juice all ingredients.

Carrot & Cabbage

    5 carrots
    ½ head cabbage

Wash and juice all ingredients.

Carrot & String Bean

5 carrots

½ cup of string beans

Wash and juice all ingredients.

Carrot & Spinach

5 carrots
1 bunch of spinach

Wash and juice all ingredients.

Green Drink

½ - 1 bunch parsley
2 - 3 sprigs watercress
2 - 3 leaves of kale

½ cucumber, (peeled, if waxed)

Wash and juice all ingredients.

Pineapple Supreme

2 rings of fresh pineapple
2 oranges, peeled

Pineapple Supreme Plus

2 rings of fresh pineapple
2 oranges, peeled
1 large grapefruit, peeled

Peel and juice all ingredients.

Citrus Wake Up

1 large grapefruit
2 oranges
1 lemon

Peel and juice all ingredients.

Note: When peeling citrus fruit, be Sure to keep the white pith on fruit. The beneficial nutrient are in the pith.

Grapefruit & Orange

2 grapefruits
1 orange

Peel and juice all ingredients.

Cranapple

2 cups fresh cranberries
2 apples

Wash and juice all ingredients.

Peach & Strawberry

2 peaches
1 cup strawberries

Pit peaches, wash and juice all ingredients.

Watermelon

2 slices of watermelon

Thoroughly wash and juice, include rind and seeds.

Section 5

Salads &
Dressings

Salads & Dressings

WEBSTER'S NINTH COLLEGIATE DICTIONARY DEFINED salads as: An incongruous mixture: Hodgepodge.

Traditionally salads have been used as a side dish or appetizer. I assure you, the following recipes will open up the world of a meal in a salad and a salad in a meal.

So You Said You Wanted A Salad*

1 head Romaine lettuce
1 bunch of parsley
1 bunch of watercress
1 bunch of arugula
1 head of red leaf lettuce
½ package or 2 bunches
   of spinach
10 grated red radishes

½ head of escarole
½ bunch of dandelion
   leaves
½ package of clover
   sprouts
½ package of alfalfa
   sprouts
garlic sesame dressing

Mix all ingredients and serve.

*Submitted by NiMaatRa Niiquerty, Professor of Purification. Heal Thyself Center

Baby Zucchini Salad

2 or more small zucchini per serving
Olive oil
Apple cider or balsamic vinegar

Cut small zucchini lengthwise into "pickles" but leave one end intact so they hold together.
Steam lightly.
Transfer to a bowl and drizzle with olive oil and vinegar.
Cool to room temperature before serving.

Asparagus Ginger Salad

1 pound asparagus, tough ends removed
6 cloves garlic, minced
1" ginger root grated, unpeeled

½ teaspoon maple syrup
2 tablespoons tamari
2 teaspoons sesame oil
1 tablespoon rice vinegar

1½ teaspoons cayenne pepper

Slice the asparagus into match sticks by cutting each stalk into 3" lengths, then slivering the lengths into thin strips with a sharp paring knife.

Steam asparagus for 5 minutes or until crisp-tender. Toss warm asparagus with remaining ingredients and serve at room temperature.

Live Food Variation: Do not steam asparagus, use raw, and marinate in sauce for one hour.

Serves 4

Couscous Salad

2 cups couscous

⅓ cup olive oil
3 tablespoons lemon juice

¼ teaspoon ground cumin

½ teaspoon honey

⅓ cup pine nuts

¼ cup fresh parsley, chopped
2 tablespoons fresh cilantro, chopped (optional)

Pour boiling water over the couscous.
Let stand five minutes.
Mix together olive oil, lemon juice, cumin and honey to make dressing.
Lightly toast pine nuts in dry heavy skillet until golden.
Fluff couscous with a fork.
Add dressing, nuts and parsley; toss together.
Top with fresh cilantro, if available.
Serve at room temperature.

Spicy Pasta Salad

2 cups cooked pasta

½ cup whole snow peas
1 red bell pepper
3 teaspoons sesame seeds

⅓ teaspoon cayenne pepper
2 tablespoons sauce
3 tablespoons sesame oil
2 tablespoons lemon juice
4 teaspoons minced garlic
4 teaspoons minced onion

Mix all ingredients with drained, cooked pasta and let marinate 30 minutes before serving.

Bean Sprout &Watercress Salad

1 pound mung bean sprouts, rinsed and dried
1 bunch watercress, rinsed, trimmed and dried
2 tablespoons balsamic vinegar
2 tablespoons natural soy sauce
1 tablespoon peanut oil
2 teaspoons roasted sesame oil
1 clove garlic, pressed

Mix sprouts and watercress in a salad bowl.
Whisk remaining ingredients together in a small bowl.
Just before serving, pour dressing over salad and toss.

Carrot Salad

Dressing:

> 4½ tablespoons orange juice
>
> ¾ teaspoon cinnamon
>
> 2½ tablespoons lemon juice
>
> 1½ teaspoons olive oil
>
> ¾ teaspoon kelp
> 3 tablespoons almond oil
>
> 1½ teaspoons maple syrup

Salad:

> 4½ cups peeled carrots, grated
>
> ¾ cup raw sunflower seeds (soak overnight)

Blend dressing ingredients together and set aside.

Toss the salad ingredients.

Toss salad with dressing.

Garnish with fresh parsley sprigs.

Serves 6

Eggplant Salad

2 medium eggplants (about 2 pounds)

2 tomatoes, coarsely chopped

1 small red onion, minced (½ cup)

1 clove garlic, minced

3 tablespoons lemon juice

2 teaspoons olive oil

1 tablespoon minced parsley

1 tablespoon minced fresh coriander

¾ teaspoon ground cumin

½ teaspoon paprika

¼ teaspoon turmeric

coriander leaves (garnish)

Trim the eggplants and cut in half lengthwise.
Place on a cookie sheet, cut side down, and bake at 400° F. for 45 minutes, or until soft to the touch. (Or grill over hot coals until soft; exact time will depend on the heat of the coals.)

Remove from oven and set aside until cool enough to handle. Scrape the pulp from the skin; discard skin. Chop pulp coarsely. Place in a large bowl. Add the tomatoes, onion, garlic, lemon juice, oil, parsley, coriander, cumin, paprika and turmeric. Stir well to combine. Cover and chill.

Garnish with coriander.

Live Food Variation: Cube raw eggplant, add remaining ingredients, cover and chill.

Serves 6

Two Bean Salad with Fresh Herbs

½ pound string beans

2½ cups cooked navy beans (about 1 cup raw)
1 medium Kirby cucumber, thinly sliced
1 small red bell pepper, finely diced

¼ cup olive oil

Juice of ½ lemon, or more to taste

¼ cup chopped fresh basil

¼ cup chopped fresh parsley
1 teaspoon maple syrup

Steam string beans until tender-crisp and rinse under cool water.

Combine with remaining ingredients and toss gently.

Live Food Variation: Use raw string beans, replace navy beans with raw green peas.

Serves 6

Cauliflower & Argula Salad

4 cups cauliflorets
6 cups argula leaves
4 tablespoons extra-virgin olive oil
2 tablespoons balsamic vinegar
1 teaspoon mustard
1 teaspoon parsley flakes

Steam cauliflorets crisp-tender, about 3 - 5 minutes; cool.
Line serving platter with arugula. Mound cauliflorets in
center.
In jar with tight-fitting lid, combine remaining ingredi-
ents, shake well to mix.
Drizzle the dressing over; toss to coat well.

Live Food Variation: Use finely chopped raw cauliflower.

Serves 6

Vegetable Salad

½ green leaf or red leaf lettuce

¼ cup scallions, chopped

¼ cup radish, chopped

½ cup cucumber, chopped

½ cup tomatoes, chopped

½ cup broccoli

½ cup cauliflower

½ cup alfalfa sprouts

½ cup olive oil

¼ cup apple cider vinegar

⅛ teaspoon fresh garlic

½ teaspoon basil

¼ teaspoon paprika
pinch of cayenne pepper

Combine all vegetables into a large bowl.
Put remaining ingredients into a tight fitted jar and shake well.
Pour over vegetables and toss lightly.

Mango Strawberry Salad

3 tablespoons agar-agar flakes
2 cups apple juice
3 tablespoons maple syrup
2 cups sliced strawberries
2 mangoes, sliced
1 tablespoon lemon juice

Add the agar-agar flakes to the apple juice in a saucepan.
Bring to a boil, cover, reduce heat and simmer for 15 minutes to dissolve the agar-agar.
Cool slightly.
Add the maple syrup, strawberries, mangoes and lemon juice. Chill until set.

Gumbo Salad

1 pound okra
2 ears corn
Argula, or red leaf lettuce

Clean and cut okra. Cut corn kernels from cob.
Mix okra and corn together, toss with a teriyaki sauce.
Serve on a bed of argula or red leaf lettuce.

Serves 6

Mushroom-Spinach Salad

1¾ cups spinach
½ cup sliced mushrooms
dash of cayenne pepper
2 teaspoons onion, chopped

Mix all ingredients. Moisten with dressing of choice.

Serves 4

Black-eyed Pea Salad*

2 cups cooked black-eyed peas
1 cup peeled tomatoes, chopped
1 cup carrots, shredded
½ cup yellow squash or zucchini, chopped
1 small onion, chopped

¼ cup olive oil
¼ teaspoon basil
¼ teaspoon garlic, fresh
1 teaspoon honey, if desired
Pinch of cayenne pepper

Combine peas, tomatoes, carrots, squash, and onions in a large bowl. Put remaining ingredients into a tight fitted jar and shake well. Pour vegetable and toss to coat. Refrigerate salad for several hours until well chilled.

Live Food Variation: Replace black-eyed peas with fresh cut green beans.

*Submitted by Dorothy Simons, Elder, Professor of Purification.

Tofu Eggless Salad

½ cup mashed tofu

¼ cup fine dried onions

¼ teaspoon tumeric
2 tablespoons oil

¼ cup celery (add at the end)
1 teaspoon yellow prepared mustard

¼ teaspoon granulated garlic

⅛ teaspoon cayenne

½ cup soy mayonnaise (see recipe)

Sauté the onions with oil and seasonings.
Add the crushed tofu and continue to sauté.
Remove from heat and add the soy mayo and celery.
Cool and serve as a sandwich on whole wheat bread or
as a salad.

Serves 2

Root Salad

2 carrots, grated
2 beets, grated
2 parsnips, grated

Combine all ingredients.
Moisten with any sauce or dressing.
Serve on a bed of greens.

Sprout Salad

Combine any of the following sprouts:
>alfalfa, clover, radish, bean or sunflower

Serve on a bed of lettuce. Squeeze juice of fresh lemon or use any dressing.

Relish Salad

Fresh herbs:
>parsley, thyme or oregano, finely chopped

>1 green pepper, chopped in small pieces
>1 red pepper, chopped in small pieces
>2 ears of corn, kernels removed
>1 small onion, finely chopped

Combine all ingredients.
Moisten with the dressing of choice.
Serve on a bed of salad greens.

DRESSINGS

A good salad doesn't need any dressings ideally a little fresh lemon juice will liven up an already live meal. But, for those who cannot resist adding salad dressing, here are some healthy yet tasty alternatives

Eggless Soy Mayonnaise

1 cup soy milk
4 teaspoons honey
1-1½ cups safflower oil
4 teaspoons apple cider vinegar
⅛ teaspoon cayenne pepper

Blend first 2 ingredients slowly adding oil.
Put 2 ingredients in a bowl and whip in next 2 ingredients slowly.
As mixture stiffens add the last 2 ingredients. Mix well and chill.

Herb Vinegar

¼ cup (packed) of fresh tarragon, basil or dill, or
4 cloves peeled
garlic or ginger
2 cups vinegar

Heat vinegar to just below the boiling point.
Add herbs and place into jar; cover loosely with a towel.
Let cool. When cool, tightly cap and let sit at room temperature for one month.
Herbs may be left in or removed.

Lemon Garlic Dressing

1 cup cider or wine
   vinegar
1 cup water
2 tablespoons lemon
   juice
½ cucumber, cut in
   chunks
1 small onion, cut in
   chunks

2 garlic cloves
¼ teaspoon cayenne
   pepper (optional)
½ teaspoon celery seed
½ teaspoon dill weed
1 tablespoon parsley
   flakes

Blend all ingredients until smooth.

Refrigerate. Keeps well in refrigerator.

Makes 2½ cups.

Miso Dressing

3 tablespoons light miso

1½ cups safflower oil

½ cup apple cider vinegar

½ cup tamari

½ cup water
1 - 2 teaspoons grated fresh ginger root (unpeeled)

¼ cup honey

Blend all ingredients until smooth.

Makes 2 cups.

Sesame Garlic Dressing

4 medium or large cloves of garlic minced
2 tablespoons basil
1 teaspoon oregano
4 cup raw sesame seeds
2 cup water
2 cup of sesame oil
1 teaspoon lemon juice
Sea salt & cayenne pepper to taste

Blend all ingredients, except oil, until smooth.

Slowly add oil. As oil blends in it will thicken the dressing.

Section 6

Soups and Stews

Soups & Stews

T RADITIONAL SOUP/STEWS RECIPES ARE "HEAVY." TO HELP THE digestive process, add flax seeds to the pot.

Those of you who are on the Natural Living program. Purée all soups/stews before consuming, adding water to thin as necessary. Soups with beans will be too glassy and should be avoided or eaten occasionally if you are on the program.

Cream of Navy Bean Soup

    1 pound navy beans, soaked
    3 quarts water
    1 large yellow onion, chopped
    4 stalks celery, with tops
    2 teaspoons curry powder
    2 cups puréed tomatoes, blended
    2 tablespoons safflower oil
    soy milk
    sprouts
    spinach leaves

In large a dutch oven place beans, water, onion and celery. Cook for 1½ hours.

Add curry and tomato, cook until beans are tender, about 1 hour.

Add oil and stir. Add milk to desired consistency. Reheat and serve.

Vegetable Broth

    2 cups carrots, thinly sliced
    2 cups green pea pods
    1 onion, sliced
    6 celery tops
    6 cups water
    outside leaves of lettuce, spinach or greens
    outside leaves of cabbage, shredded

Wash vegetables, slice and put into large saucepan. Cover with water.

Bring to a boil and let simmer about ½ hour. Strain and serve.

Split Pea Soup

½ cup dry split peas
¼ cup dry lima beans
⅛ cup rice
4 cups water
1 yellow onion, chopped
1 bay leaf
½ teaspoon celery seed
1 carrot, sliced
1 stalk celery, sliced
1 potato, chopped
¼ teaspoon paprika
1 tablespoon parsley flakes (or
¼ cup chopped fresh parsley)
½ teaspoon basil
⅛ teaspoon cayenne pepper

In a large pot, combine peas, lima beans, rice, water, onion, bay leaf and celery seed.

Bring to a boil, reduce heat, cover and simmer for 1½ hours.

Add remaining ingredients, cover and simmer an additional 45 minutes.

Remove bay leaf before serving.

Serves 4

Vegetable Stew

1 pound lentils
5 cups water or vegetable broth
6 tablespoons water for sautéing
2 leeks, thinly sliced
1 clove garlic, mashed
4 carrots, thinly sliced
2 stalks celery, thinly sliced
4 large potatoes, cubed
2 small white turnips, cubed
2 cups tomatoes, peeled and drained
(fresh or canned)

½ teaspoon cayenne pepper
1 teaspoon Fines herbs
2 tablespoons fresh parsley, chopped

Cook lentils by bringing to a boil, cover and simmer about 45 minutes. Sauté leeks in water about five minutes. Add garlic, carrots, celery, potatoes and turnips. Cook 10 minutes more, stirring, over low heat. Add cooked vegetables to lentils. Add tomatoes, pepper and herbs. Simmer 20 minutes, uncovered, or until vegetables are tender. Mash some of the lentils with a potato masher if thickening is not needed. Serve hot, sprinkle with parsley.

Seaweed Vegetable Soup

4 teaspoons water, for sautéing
2 small strips kombu
1 yellow onion, sliced into thin strips
1 large carrot, sliced
1 cup orange squash (acorn or hubbard is good)
    peeled and cut into small cubes
1 cup broccoli florets
3 cups water seasoned with tamari, pepper or
    nutritional yeast
Freshly minced parsley for garnish

Heat water in soup pot and add kombu (keep in strips). Stir in onion.
Sauté over medium high heat until onion is soft but not browned.
Add carrot, squash and broccoli.
Cook for two minutes.
Add seasoned water, basil and marjoram and bring to a boil.
Lower heat to medium and cook, covered, for 20 minutes or until squash is soft. Season with tamari and garnish with parsley.
Before serving, slice kombu into thin strips and serve in soup.

Serves 4 - 6

Zucchini Soup

1 onion
4 cups water
4 large zucchini, cut in chunks
⅓ cup fresh dill, finely chopped
2 tablespoons soy sauce
dash of garlic powder

Cook the onion in ½ cups of water in a medium saucepan for five minutes.
Add the remaining water, and the rest of the ingredients.
Bring to a boil, reduce heat, cover and simmer about 20 minutes. Process in blender, small amounts at a time, until velvety smooth. Serve warm.

Serves 6

Carrot Soup

3 large carrots, chopped
1 small onion, chopped
1 potato, peeled and chopped
4 cups water
¼ teaspoon ground ginger
⅛ teaspoon ground nutmeg
1 teaspoon lemon juice

Combine all ingredients in a saucepan.
Bring to a boil, reduce heat, cover and
 simmer for 15 minutes.
In a blender or food processor, blend soup until smooth. Return to pan and heat through.
Garnish with chopped fresh parsley or coriander.

Serves 4

Potato Leek Soup

3 tablespoons soy margarine
1 cup minced onion
3 cups sliced potatoes
1 cup sliced celery
1 cup sliced leeks
2 cups thinly sliced carrots
4 cups water
1 teaspoon maple syrup

Melt margarine in a large skillet.
Add the potatoes and onion, and sauté gently
for about five minutes, stirring to prevent sticking.
Add the leeks, half the carrots and celery and the
water. Bring to a boil, then reduce heat and simmer
gently for about 20 minutes, stirring occasionally.
Meanwhile, steam the remaining carrots until tender.
When the potato-leek mixture is cooked, purée
it in a blender.
If the purée is too thick, add water to thin it, then add
the maple syrup.
Reheat before serving.
Float some of the steamed carrot slices on each serving.

Serves 4

HEAL THYSELF NATURAL LIVING COOK BOOK

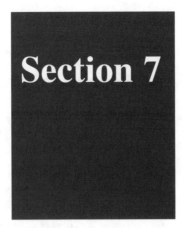

Section 7

Marinade/Sauces Dips

Marinade/Sauces & Dips

THE GREAT THING ABOUT MARINADE, SAUCE OR DIP IS THAT they add a zip to any veggie, pasta or tofu dish. Use on raw, steamed grilled or sautéed vegetables, tofu or tempeh

Sesame Sauce

3 tablespoons sesame paste
4 tablespoons soy sauce
1 tablespoon sesame oil

In a bowl slowly add soy sauce to tahini and blend well.
Stir in sesame oil.

Hoisin Sauce

¼ cup miso
2 teaspoons toasted sesame oil
¼ cup honey
1 teaspoon soy sauce
2 tablespoons water
1½ teaspoons apple cider vinegar

Combine all ingredients and mix well.

Tofu Cottage Cheese

1 cup mashed tofu
½ cup onion, chopped fine
3 teaspoons water for sautéing
¼ teaspoon dillweed
½ cup soy mayonnaise (see recipe)
2 tablespoons chopped chives

Sauté the onions in the water with the seasonings. Cool.
Add the mashed tofu, chives and soy mayo.

Cool and serve as a salad.

Makes 2 cups

Gingery Tahini Sauce

½ cup tahini sauce
1 tablespoon mustard
1 tablespoon miso
1 teaspoon ginger juice
1 tablespoon rice or umeboshi vinegar

1½ - 2 cups water

Purée all ingredients in blender until smooth. In a saucepan, heat slowly over a low flame, do not boil! Add water to obtain desired consistency. Tastes great over noodles.

Creamy Tofu Dip with Garlic & Dill

8 ounces soft tofu
3 tablespoons lemon juice
2 tablespoons safflower oil
1 tablespoon tamari (or to taste)
3 large cloves garlic

1½ teaspoons dill weed

1½ teaspoons parsley, finely minced

In a blender, blend lemon juice and garlic until garlic is minced very fine.
Add remaining ingredients except parsley and purée until smooth.
Stir in parsley.

Mustard Marinade

2 tablespoons dijon-style mustard

3 cloves garlic, crushed

3 tablespoons tamari or soy sauce

3 tablespoons Lemon or lime juice

1 tablespoon vegetable oil

Mix all ingredients except oil.
Add the oil ½ teaspoon at a time, mixing vigorously after each addition.

Makes 5 ounces

Sweet & Tangy Marinade

3 tablespoons vegetable oil

½ cup cider vinegar

¾ cup ketchup

¼ cup soy sauce

1 tablespoon molasses

3 tablespoons maple syrup

Pinch allspice

Bring all ingredients to a boil, cover, reduce heat and simmer 5 minutes. Cool.

Makes 2 cups

Apple Ginger Marinade

¼ cup apple juice or cider
1 tablespoon minced fresh ginger

¼ cup cider vinegar

⅓ cup vegetable oil

⅓ cup tamari

⅓ cup honey
2 cloves garlic, crushed

Mix all ingredients.

Homemade Teriyaki Sauce

½ cup tamari or soy sauce

¼ cup rice vinegar
1 tablespoon sake, mirin or white wine (optional)
1 tablespoon rice syrup or honey
dash hot pepper sauce
1 teaspoon toasted sesame oil

Whisk together ingredients.

Makes 1 cup.

Mustard

¼ cup ground brown mustard seeds
3 tablespoons boiling water
1 tablespoon olive oil

¼ teaspoon maple syrup

Mix all ingredients together.

Tofu "Sour Cream"

½ pound tofu
2 - 3 tablespoons lemon juice

¼ herbal seasoning
3 tablespoons oil
water

Blend all ingredients, except oil, until creamy.
Gradually add oil while still blending.
For tartness add more lemon juice. If too thick, add a little water.

Makes 1 cup

Spirulina Sauce

4 tablespoons water for sautéing
1 onion, chopped
2 cloves garlic, minced
4 cups assorted fresh vegetables, chopped
2 tablespoons whole wheat flour
1 tablespoon spirulina

Sauté onion and garlic in water for 5 minutes, or until soft.
Slightly steam vegetables.
Dilute the flour in the water.
Simmer until thickened.
Stir in spirulina.
Pour sauce over steamed vegetables.

Soy Mayonnaise

1½ pounds tofu
¾ cup oil
2 tablespoons apple cider vinegar
1 cup water
1 tablespoon mustard
¼ teaspoon granulated garlic
⅛ medium onion
½ teaspoon cayenne pepper (optional)
2 tablespoons lemon juice
1 tablespoon cashew meal (optional if using a firmer tofu)

Blend all ingredients until smooth.

Section 8

Main
Dishes

Main Dishes

ONE OF THE MAIN THINGS I LEARNED OVER THE YEARS IS, that as a vegetarian, I didn't have to give up all of the foods I grew up on. Many recipes could be adapted without the meat, and there are alternatives for salt, sugar and oil.

One of my favorite stories, is of a Super Bowl party that I would have every year with lots of food. Being the only vegetarian, the regulars were used to eating a vegetarian meal. I always gave them the option of bringing a meat dish if they had to have meat, (no one ever did!). One year I decided to make chili. I used tofu that had been frozen, thawed and crumbled to give a ground beef texture. As the hostess, I was the last to begin eating. As I did a few of my guests stopped and looked at me in disbelief. I knew immediately what was on their minds. I smiled and said, "that's tofu, not ground beef you're eating." Everyone was amazed that they could not tell the difference!

A word of caution, many of our favorite meals even with the adaptations are still too "heavy" for a *natural living* diet. Always limit how often you eat grains, nuts and beans. Many of the following recipes call for serving over rice or noodles. As you progress on your *natural living* diet, fix the recipe but omit the grain or noodle and use the live food variation.

If you are in transition from a meat based diet to a vegetarian diet or cook for meat eaters, these recipes will be a refreshing change.

Curry Mixed Vegetables

2 cups cooked brown rice
1 cup string beans cut in thirds
2 cups shredded cabbage
1 onion, chopped
4 cloves of garlic
1 cup mushrooms, sliced

1 cup ginger tea (1 teaspoon ginger, ½ orange peel)
1 large green pepper
3 tablespoons curry (to taste)
1 tablespoon soy sauce
pinch of cayenne (to taste)

Heat pan. Put garlic, onion, green pepper, mushrooms
and tea (enough to cover vegetables) in pan.
Simmer until mushrooms are tender.
Add soy sauce and curry.
Stir well.
Add remaining vegetables and tea. Steam until vegetables
turn bright green, approximately 5 minutes.
Add rice. Stir well.

Tofu Creole

⅔ cup vegetable oil
½ cup flour
1¾ cups shallots (scal-
lions), thinly sliced
⅓ cup chopped celery
1 cup chopped onion
½ cup chopped green
pepper
4 teaspoons garlic, fine-
ly minced
1 to 1½ pounds Italian
style whole peeled
tomatoes
1- 8 ounces jar tomato
sauce:
1 tablespoon minced
chives

4 whole bay leaves,
crushed
6 whole allspice:
2 whole cloves
½ teaspoon cayenne
¼ teaspoon chili powder
¼ teaspoon mace:
¼ teaspoon dried basil
½ teaspoon dried
thyme:
4 teaspoons fresh lemon
juice
2 cups water
2 pounds cubed tofu,
thawed

In a heavy 6 - 8 quart pot or kettle, heat oil and
gradually add flour, stirring constantly.
Cook over low heat, stirring constantly, until a
 medium brown roux (the color of rich peanut butter)
if formed. Remove from the heat, add fresh vegetables
and parsley. Mix well with the roux, then return to low
heat and cook, stirring constantly, until the vegetables
begin to brown.
Mix in canned tomatoes and tomato sauce, then add
chives, seasonings, lemon juice and mix again.
Raise the heat under the pan and bring to a low boil.
Add water and mix thoroughly. When the mixture
boils up again, reduce the heat and simmer
for 45 minutes. Add the tofu and allow to come to a

low boil again, then cover, reduce heat slightly and simmer for 20 minutes. Remove the pot from the burner and allow to stand covered, at room temperature for about 10 minutes before serving. Serve over brown rice.

Stuffed Squash

2 medium acorn squash
2 medium carrots, chopped
2 tablespoons maple syrup
1 teaspoon cinnamon and nutmeg

Cut squash in ½ and clean out seeds.
Place cut side down in baking dish. Cover.
Bake at 350° F for 30 minutes.
Turn cut side up, bake for 30 minutes longer. Scoop pulp out of each half, keeping shells intact.
Place cooked pulp in bowl and set aside.
Meanwhile, steam carrots until tender.
Add to cooked squash pulp.
Mix together until mashed.
Stir in maple syrup, cinnamon and nutmeg.
Spoon into reserved squash shells.
Bake, uncovered, at 350° F for 15 minutes.

Serves 8

Dandelion Greens*

2 pounds dandelion greens
2 tablespoons olive oil

½ teaspoon cayenne
ginger
tahini (sesame)
herbs
2 tablespoons water

Remove roots and pick over carefully, washing in water several times.
Dry between paper towels.
Heat water, stir in greens, cover wok or skillet tightly; steam for 10 minutes over low heat.
Add olive oil, chop, season accordingly and serve.
Top with sesame tahini.

Serves 4

* Submitted by Rabiah Latif, Professor of Purification.

Kale (Steamed)

Boiling water
fresh kale

½ teaspoon cayenne
lemon juice

½ teaspoon caraway seeds or ground ginger tahini
(sesame)

Remove roots and clean thoroughly, dry between paper towels. Chill until ready to use. Tear into shreds if leaves are large.

Drop into a little water along with seasonings, cover and steam 5 -6 minutes.

Add lemon juice top with sesame tahini and serve.

Turnip Greens

2 pounds turnip greens
2 cups water
2 tablespoons safflower oil
2 cubes vegetable bouillon
1 clove garlic, chopped
1 large red onion, chopped
1 teaspoon soy sauce

½ teaspoon basil
1 bay leaf

⅛ teaspoon dill

¼ teaspoon oregano
1 tablespoon soy margarine

Wash greens and cut into tiny pieces.
Bring water to a boil in saucepan.
Add bouillon cubes.
Simmer until the cubes dissolve.
Place greens in a large skillet or wok.
Cover with seasoned water.
Add remaining ingredients.
Cover and simmer until tender 10 - 15 minutes.
Add oil after greens have cooked and remove bay leaf.

Serves 4

Ratatouille

3 cups eggplant, cubed
2 cups zucchini, sliced
1 green pepper, chopped
1 clove garlic, minced

¼ cup olive oil

¼ cup water
2 tablespoons fresh chopped parsley
2 tomatoes, chopped

Combine all ingredients except the parsley, oil and tomatoes in a skillet and cook covered over medium heat 10 - 15 minutes until the vegetables are tender.
Add the parsley and tomatoes.
Cook another 5 minutes.
Remove from heat, add oil and stir well.
Serve hot or cold.

Live Food Variation: Do not cook vegetables, mix all ingredients and marinate for at least 2 hours.

Serves 6

Savory Daikon

4 - 6 ½ tablespoons water
4 cups daikon or turnip, coarsely shredded
   (loosely packed)
1 tablespoon soy sauce
large pinch date sugar or drop of maple syrup
2 teaspoons green onion, minced

Heat water over a high flame.
When water is hot, add daikon or turnip, lower heat to medium-high or medium, stir-fry 32 minutes.
While cooking, mash vegetable frequently and firmly to ensure even, complete cooking.
Remove from heat and sprinkle with soy sauce, date sugar, and onion.
Mix and mash another minute or so.
Serve warm.

Serves 3 - 4

Avocado Supreme

2 - 3 ripe avocados, sliced
1 tomato, cut in wedges
1 bunch of scallions, finely chopped
1 small garlic, minced
1 lemon, juiced

⅛ teaspoon kelp

Mix all ingredients and serve on a bed of fresh greens.

Marinated Broccoli & Cauliflower

½ pound fresh broccoli

½ head of cauliflower

¼ cup apple cider vinegar

2 teaspoons lemon juice

1 teaspoon basil

1 teaspoon dill

Wash vegetables and cut them into flowers.
In a bowl combine ingredients add vegetables and
marinate 5 - 7 hours in a covered glass dish in the
refrigerator.
Serve at room temperature.

Cauliflower Pilaf

1 head of cauliflower

1 scallion, finely chopped

1 ear of corn, raw, kernels removed

1 red pepper, finely chopped

1 green pepper, finely chopped

Fresh herbs, to taste

In a food processor, chop cauliflower
until its the consistency of a grain.
Mix all ingredients.
Add dressing or sauce to moisten.
Serve on a bed of lettuce or grated carrots.

Seaweed Gumbo

2 pounds okra

½ package hiziki seaweed

½ package mekabu or wakame seaweed
2 bay leaves

½ cup chopped parsley
4 cups boiling water
2 green peppers, chopped
5 ripe tomatoes
1 package black mushrooms
1 package oyster mushrooms
1 large chopped onion

¼ teaspoon thyme

¼ cup water
2 cups chopped celery
cayenne pepper (to taste)

Sauté onions, pepper, celery in water.
Chop and sauté okra; cook until okra is bright green.
Purée tomatoes and add to onions, celery and peppers.
Soak seaweed in water, then cut in bite-sized pieces.
Simmer tomato mixture for 15 minutes, then
add boiling water.
Add mushrooms, seaweed, cayenne, thyme and parsley.
Cook at a low simmer for 3 - 4 hours, adding okra ½
hour before serving.
Serve over rice.

Tofu Stuffed Peppers

5 ounces water
1 onion, chopped
1 garlic clove, chopped
14 ounces tofu, squeezed and mashed or
2 ounces wild rice, cooked
1 teaspoon oregano

½ teaspoon basil
4 red peppers, medium cayenne pepper

Heat water and sauté the onions and garlic
until transparent.
Add the crumbled tofu or wild rice, oregano and basil.
Cook ingredients for 5 minutes, stirring constantly to
avoid burning the onions.
Add cayenne pepper, set aside to cool slightly.
Cut off the bottoms of the peppers, remove seeds and
wash the peppers.
Fill the peppers with the tofu mixture and steam them
for 10 - 16 minutes or until the stuffing is
heated through.

**Live Food Variation: Replace wild rice or tofu with finely
chopped cauliflower and grated carrots. Combine all
ingredients—do not sauté garlic or onions—and stuff
peppers.**

Sesame String Beans

1 pound string beans
1 clove garlic, crushed
½ cup water
4 tablespoons sesame oil
3 tablespoons apple cider vinegar
½ teaspoon cayenne pepper
½ cup toasted sesame seeds

Steam beans until bright green and somewhat crisp. Douse in ice water and let them sit until chilled, changing water if necessary.

In a small skillet, sauté the garlic in water.

Add sesame oil, vinegar and pepper.

Heat gently for several minutes until mixture is hot. Meanwhile, toast sesame seeds in a cast iron skillet until brown.

No oil is needed, but watch the seeds carefully, since they tend to burn easily.

Drain beans and pat dry.

Toss with hot oil mixture and sesame seeds.

Serve immediately.

Live Food Variation: Use raw string beans. Combine remaining ingredients—without heating—and marinate for at least 1 hour.

serves 4

Grilled Corn on The Cob

⅓ cup soy margarine, softened
1½ tablespoons minced fresh parsley leaves
1½ tablespoons snipped fresh chives
1½ tablespoons fresh thyme
1½ tablespoons minced scallion
1 teaspoon fresh lemon juice
8 ears of fresh corn
hot sauce to taste

Combine all ingredients except corn in a bowl.
Let stand at least 1 hour or overnight.
Let mixture soften to a spreadable consistency.
Peel back but do not remove the husks from the corn and discard the silk.
Spread each ear with two teaspoons of the herb butter, wrap the husks carefully around the corn and wrap each ear in foil.
Roast the corn on a grill over hot coals, turning occasionally, for about 20 minutes or until the kernels are tender.
Unwrap the corn, remove the husks and serve hot.

Rice Mushroom Casserole

1 cup brown rice

2 onions, chopped

½ pound mushrooms, chopped

2 cups boiling water

½ teaspoon thyme

¼ teaspoon garlic powder

½ tablespoons soy sauce

2 tablespoons wheat germ

Sauté onions in one-quarter cup for 10 minutes.

Add mushrooms to pot and cook five minutes longer.

Add rice, cook and stir for five minutes longer.

Remove from heat.

Add two cups boiling water, seasonings and wheat germ.

Mix well.

Pour into a casserole dish, cover, and bake in a 350° F oven for 1¼ hours.

Serve plain or with a sauce.

This dish may be prepared ahead; add 30 minutes to baking time.

Serves 6

Vegetarian Paella

1 cup uncooked brown basmati rice
2 cups boiling water
3 teaspoons water
½ cup chopped onion
3 cloves garlic, minced
½ cup each: sliced green bell pepper and sliced red
    bell pepper
½ cup diced tomato
2 small red potatoes, thinly sliced
2 cups hot water flavored with soy sauce and fresh
    herbs
1 teaspoon saffron
¾ teaspoon oregano
5 marinated artichoke hearts
1 cup peas (fresh or frozen)*

Let rice stand for 20 minutes in water, then drain.
In a large, heavy skillet, heat water and sauté onion and
garlic until onion is soft.
Add bell peppers, tomato and potatoes.
Sauté vegetables, about 3 minutes.
Add rice and flavored water.
Bring to a boil, then lower heat to simmer.
Add saffron and oregano.
Cover pot and let simmer until rice is tender (about 35
minutes for brown basmati).
Arrange artichokes and peas on top of rice,
(* if you cannot find fresh peas, buy frozen peas with no salt
added. There are organic frozen peas in your local health food
store.)
Cover and cook until peas turn bright green, about 1
minute.

Serve hot.

Serves 8

Main Dishes

Vegetable Pulao Rice

2½ cups basmati rice

¼ cup water

1 medium onion, diced

6 - 8 cloves

2 bay leaves

6 - 8 black peppercorns

1 teaspoon cumin seeds

1 two-inch long cinnamon stick

½ teaspoon finely ground chili powder

½ cup green peas

½ cup diced carrots

2½ pints of water

Wash the rice and drain.
Put water in a saucepan over medium heat.
When the water gets hot, add cloves, black peppercorns, cumin seeds, cinnamon stick, bay leaves and stir for a minute.
Add onions, carrots, peas and chili powder.
Stir for another 5 minutes.
Reduce heat and add rice followed by water.
Bring it to a boil and reduce to medium heat until the water is absorbed.
Then cover and let cook on simmer for 20 minutes until the rice gets tender, soft and fluffy.

NOODLE BASED DISHES

Sweet 'n' Sour Noodles

1 package clear noodles, somen or udon
3 teaspoons water for sautéing
2 slices ginger root, peeled
1 medium onion, thinly sliced
2 ribs celery, thinly sliced
2 medium carrots, thinly sliced
1 small red or green bell pepper, seeded and sliced
2 cups bite-sized broccoli florets and stalks
½ to ⅔ cup water
¼ cup rice vinegar
3 tablespoons maple syrup
1 tablespoon soy sauce
1 - 1½ tablespoons arrowroot dissolved in an equal
   amount of water

Cook noodles according to package directions and rinse until cool.

Sauté ginger, celery, onion, carrot and bell pepper in hot water for 2 - 3 minutes.

Cover and cook 5 minutes. Add broccoli, cover and cook about 5 minutes more (until broccoli is just tender but still bright green).

Uncover pan, remove from heat, and discard the ginger. In small saucepan, combine water, vinegar, maple syrup and soy sauce. Bring the mixture to a gentle simmer, then remove from heat. Slowly pour in dissolved arrowroot stirring briskly. Return pan to heat and simmer for 1 - 2 minutes, stirring constantly. Mix the sauce with the vegetables and serve over the noodles.

Variation: Add 1 pound tofu cubed, adding tofu when broccoli is added. Serve without noodles.

Serves 2

Baked Macaroni And Cheese

1 cup nutritional yeast
⅓ cup whole wheat flour
2 cups water
1 large onion
½ cup soy margarine
2 teaspoons mustard
3½ cups cooked elbow macaroni
pinch of paprika

Mix the dry ingredients together in a saucepan. Gradually add the water making a smooth paste by beating the mixture with a whisk.
Continue to add water until the paste is thinned out. Place on a medium to low heat and stir constantly with a whisk until it thickens and bubbles.
Let it bubble for 30 seconds and remove from heat. Whip in the margarine and mustard and grated onion. Mix half of the sauce with the drained macaroni and put in casserole dish.
Put remaining macaroni and sauce on top.
Sprinkle with paprika and bake for 15 minutes
in a 350° F preheated oven.
Put in broiler for a few minutes until "cheese" sauce is stretchy and crisp.

Serves 6 - 8

This is a very *heavy* dish. It should be prepared on rare occasions. Next time you're having your family that can not eat without at least one of the "traditional" dishes, serve this.

To help digest heavy starch meals, drink juice of one lemon with warm water ½ hour prior to meal.

Noodles With Sesame-Ginger Sauce

1 package udon, somen or soba (or any pasta)

¼ cup water

¼ cup tahini

1½ teaspoons soy sauce
1 tablespoons Lemon juice
1 tablespoon mirin (optional)

¼ cup water
1 tablespoon Lemon juice
1 tablespoon juice of grated ginger root
1 small clove garlic, finely minced

Cook noodles according to package directions, rinse until cool.

In a medium sized saucepan, add ¼ cup water to tahini a little at a time, mixing well to form a smooth sauce. Add all remaining ingredients; bring to a simmer over medium heat.

Gently simmer 1 minute. (The sauce will thicken as it cooks. If it becomes too thick, add a little water.)

Ladle sauce over noodles in individual serving

Pasta & Broccoli

12 ounces whole wheat pasta
Water for boiling
1 pound broccoli, cut
2 large cloves garlic, minced

¼- ½ teaspoon cayenne

3½ cups diced fresh tomatoes

Cook pasta in boiling water until tender.
Steam broccoli until tender-crisp, about 3 minutes. Set aside.
In a large skillet sauté garlic and cayenne in water for 1 minute.
Add tomatoes and cook over medium heat for 5 -10 minutes.
Add broccoli.
Serve over cooked pasta.

Serves 6-8

Tofu Mexican Style

1 onion, chopped fine
1 green bell pepper,
  chopped medium
1 red bell pepper, chopped
  medium
1 pound firm tofu, crumbled
  (*squeeze out excess water*)
½ teaspoon oregano
½ teaspoon chili powder
½ teaspoon cumin powder

¼ teaspoon black pepper,
  finely ground
½ teaspoon tumeric powder
⅛ teaspoon cayenne pepper,
  finely ground
2 cups whole tomatoes,
  blanched, seeded and
  diced
6 tablespoons water

Steam the vegetables for several minutes.
In a separate pan, simmer tomatoes and tofu with seasonings.
Add steamed vegetables and serve.

Serves 4

Tofu Loaf

28 ounces firm tofu, drained and mashed
1⅔ cups rolled oats
¾ cup whole wheat bread crumbs
⅓ cup ketchup
5 tablespoons soy sauce
2 tablespoons dijon mustard
¼ teaspoon garlic powder (optional)
¼ teaspoon cayenne pepper (optional)

Combine all ingredients in a large bowl. Mix well. Press mixture into a lightly oiled loaf pan. Bake at 350° F for 1 hour. Let cool for 15 minutes, then remove from pan.

Tofu with Ginger & Onion

16 ounces regular or firm tofu
2 teaspoons ginger root, minced
1 tablespoon green onion, minced, or
3 tablespoons soy sauce
2 teaspoons sesame oil

Cut the tofu into one-inch cubes and place in a bowl. Toss gently, using chopsticks, with the remaining ingredients.
Toss two or three times at intervals until the dressing is absorbed. This should take only a few minutes at most.

TIP To remove excess water from tofu, drain tofu and press between two plates (add weight to top plate if necessary)

Curried Tofu

1 onion, chopped
2 cloves garlic, minced
5 tablespoons water
1 teaspoon curry powder

1 pound tofu, drained and
cubed
1 cup peas
1 carrot, diced
1 celery, diced

Sauté onion and garlic in water.
Add remaining ingredients and cook over medium heat for 10 - 20 minutes, adding extra water if needed to prevent sticking. Serve.

Serves 4

Tofu & Cherry Tomato KeBobs

    1 bottle natural barbecue sauce
    1 tablespoon miso
    1½ cakes tofu, cut into cubes slightly smaller than
         the cherry tomatoes
    1 pint cherry tomatoes

In a medium bowl, combine the barbecue sauce
and miso.
Add the tofu cubes and marinate for at least and hour,
turning occasionally.
To grill, alternate the tofu cubes and cherry tomatoes on
greased bamboo or metal skewers.
Grill over hot coals for 10 15 minutes, turning occasionally.

Serves 4 - 6

Tempeh Jambalaya

½ pound tempeh, cut into ½ inch squares
1 large onion, chopped
2 - 5 cloves garlic, minced
2 carrots, diced, about 1 cup
1 green pepper, diced
2 stalks celery, chopped
2 teaspoons water
2 bay leaves
1 cup long grain brown rice
2 cups water
pinch each of the following seasonings:
    cayenne, oregano, chili powder
    cloves, nutmeg or mace
chopped parsley or scallions for garnish

Cut tempeh into squares.
In a skillet, sauté tempeh in water about 3 minutes.
Set aside.
In a heavy pot with a tight fitting lid heat the 2 teaspoons water.
Add the vegetables; sauté for a few minutes .
Add tempeh, spices and rice; stir to coat.
Next, add water and stir again, Cover, bring mixture to a boil, lower heat, simmer (or pressure cook) for 45 minutes, until liquid is absorbed.
Fluff with a fork and garnish with parsley or scallions.

Serves 4 - 6

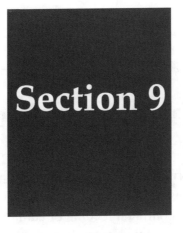

Section 9

Children's Menu

Children's Menu

ANY PARENT OF A SMALL CHILD WILL TELL YOU THEIR CHILD either does not like meat or will eat very little meat. It is only with continual feeding of adult preferences that children develop such tastes. Remember processed baby foods used to be made with salt and sugar for the mother's taste buds, not the child's. If we enhance our child's natural instinct and guide them in developing sound healthy eating habits, we have given them the greatest gift!

The concern most parents have is what about my children. Will they eat a vegetarian diet? Will they eat all they need? Will they succumb to peer pressure?

Children adapt easily. If they are raised from birth as vegetarians, with a healthy outlook they will flourish and grow.

If the family is making the transition to vegetarianism, be mindful that if it's hard on you sometimes, it will be the same for your children.

The key is to communicate with your child the reasons why you've chosen this lifestyle. Remember the growing process is to challenge and experiment. By being flexible and creative your child can still experiment within acceptable limits.

Golden Rule: *If you don't want your child eating certain foods you __must not__ eat those foods or have them in your home.*

One day Kali-my 3½ year old from birth vegan-came home from school and told me she did not want to be a vegetarian anymore. When I asked why she said because gum had sugar in it and

HEAL THYSELF NATURAL LIVING COOK BOOK

she wanted to chew gum. I told her she could still be a vegetarian and chew gum that didn't have sugar in it. We went to the health food store and purchased sugarless chewing gum (of course I was cringing inside during this whole episode). Kali chewed it and told me it tasted bad. The subject has never come up again.

The following recipes are suitable for lunches.

SANDWICHES

Pocket Fillers

Whole wheat pita pockets are excellent to pack in a child's or adult's lunch.

Any of the following spreads can be used. Add sprouts, cucumbers, lettuce or tomatoes.

REMEMBER. As you make progress on your diet, breads should be eaten sparingly and eventually omitted. All of these sandwiches can be eaten without bread. Use on greens or eat alone. Fillings can be carried in a tight fitting container.

Veggie Pocket

Grated carrots, and/or beets with sprouts, lettuce and cucumbers. Add raw or roasted sesame seeds.

Variations: The veggie pocket can be made without the pita bread.

Sesame Spread

⅓ cup sesame butter
2 tablespoons chopped sunflower seeds

Mix together all ingredients and spread on toasted whole wheat bread.

Variation: Spread on a large rice cake or serve on a bed of lettuce.

Tofu Spread

½ pound tofu

½ teaspoon grated lemon peel
1 - 2 tablespoons lemon juice
1 - 2 tablespoons honey

Combine and mash all ingredients well with a fork, or purée in a food processor.
Serve on a bed of salad greens with grated carrots or beets.

Makes 1½ Cups

Guacamole

2 medium avocados, peeled and mashed
1 tomato, finely chopped
   (peel for a smoother consistency)
1 tablespoon minced onion
1 tablespoon chopped fresh cilantro or parsley
1 tablespoon fresh lemon juice

Combine all ingredients in a wooden or ceramic bowl (do not use metal or it will cause discoloration in the avocado).
Mix well.
Serve on a bed of lettuce with grated carrots or beets.

Humus

1½ cups raw chickpeas, cooked and cooled
2 large cloves garlic
2 teaspoon tamari
Juice from 2 medium lemons

½ - ¾ cup tahini (sesame butter)

⅛ cup minced parsley
3 tablespoons red onion, finely minced

Use as a spread on rice cakes or to fill a pita pocket.

NOTE: Nori sheets, sushi, can make an excellent substitute for sandwich bread

Sushi Roll-ups

2 cups cooked short-grain brown rice
4 sheets nori, lightly toasted
1 green onion, sliced lengthwise into 4 strips
1 red bell pepper, sliced into 16 thin strips
8 leaves fresh spinach

¼ cup sesame seeds, lightly toasted,

(reserve ⅛ teaspoon for garnish)

Place one sheet of nori on a clean dishtowel or sushi mat, and spoon ½ cup rice on top.

Spread rice evenly to edges of nori. Line a strip onion, four strips of bell pepper and two spinach leaves in center.

Sprinkle with sesame seeds.

Roll into a tight roll and press to seal edges.

Slice into pieces.

Variations: Use mashed tofu, shredded carrots, beets and mashed avocado to replace brown rice. Better yet. use the pulp from your juicer as a filler.

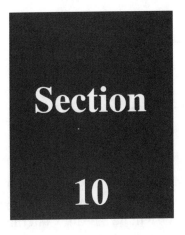

Section

10

Desserts

Desserts

Oʜ! Do I ʜᴀᴠᴇ ᴛᴏ ɢɪᴠᴇ ᴜᴘ ᴀʟʟ ᴍʏ ɢᴏᴏᴇʏ, sᴜɢᴀʀʏ ᴅᴇssᴇʀᴛs?
For a healthier lifestyle, yes you do! However, I think the following recipes will be a healthy alternative while you make
the transition. They will spur you on to create your own
healthy alternatives and have some fun doing so.

But, remember, desserts no matter how healthy should be
eaten occasionally.

Tahini Cookies

Dry Ingredients:

   3 cups whole wheat pastry flour

Liquid Ingredients:

   1 pound tahini sauce

   ⅔ cup liquid lecithin

   ¾ cup maple syrup
   1 teaspoon vanilla extract

Sift flour into a mixing bowl.

In a separate bowl, cream tahini sauce, maple syrup and vanilla together until smooth.

Add flour to tahini mixture and stir to mix evenly.

Preheat oven to 350° F.

Lightly oil cookie sheet.

Form dough into walnut sized balls, and press with a fork.

Bake 10 - 15 minutes, until light brown. Cookies will be crumbly while hot.

Allow to cool 10 minutes, then remove from tray.

Makes 30 small cookies.

Ginger Cookies

½ cup molasses
1 tablespoon liquid lecithin

½ teaspoon baking soda
1 teaspoon hot water

1½ teaspoons ground ginger

½ teaspoon cinnamon

1¾ cups whole wheat flour

Combine molasses, lecithin, baking soda dissolved in hot water, ginger and cinnamon.

Add enough flour to make a dough firm enough to roll; use your hands if necessary.

Roll thinly on a floured surface and cut into shapes with a cookie cutter.

Place on a greased baking sheet and bake at 350° F for about 10 minutes.

Transfer to a wire rack to cool.

Makes 2 dozen cookies.

1 cup grated carrots
1 cup raisins
½ cup honey
¼ cup chopped dates
1 teaspoon cinnamon
1 teaspoon allspice
½ teaspoon nutmeg

¼ teaspoon ground
  cloves
1¾ cups water
1½ cups whole wheat
  flour
1 teaspoon. baking soda
½ cup bran

Almond Cookies

¾ cup almonds
2 tablespoons liquid lecithin

¼ cup real maple syrup

¾ teaspoon vanilla

¼ teaspoon almond extract

¼ teaspoon cinnamon

⅔ cup rolled oats
2 tablespoons water

Preheat oven to 350° F.
Use a food processor or a blender to make
the cookie batter.
First, process the almonds until coarsely chopped.
Add remaining ingredients except water and pulse
briefly to mix.
Turn machine on and add 1½ - 2 tablespoons water, or
just enough to moisten.
Scrape down the sides of the machine and mix again.
Use a spoon to pat out 10 cookie rounds onto a greased
baking sheet.
Bake about 25 minutes, until light brown. Remove
immediately from pan using a metal spatula.

No-Bake Blueberry Couscous Cake*

5 cups apple or apricot juice
1 lemon, juiced and rind grated
1 pint blueberries
2 cups couscous

Bring juice to a boil in a sauce pan, add lemon rind and lemon juice.
Add two cups of couscous, pouring in slowly and constantly to prevent lumping.
Stir until couscous has absorbed juice and becomes thick; this will take about two or three minutes.
Add rinsed blueberries, allowing the heat to soften them; this takes about one minute. Some berries will burst, giving blue streaks to the cake.
Rinse a glass or ceramic baking dish; pour the cake mix into the damp dish.
Allow to cool and cut into squares.
Glaze top with a fruit jelly.

Maple Soy Frosting

1 cup soy milk powder

½ cup maple syrup
2 tablespoons vanilla
3 tablespoons orange juice

Combine all ingredients and beat until smooth and creamy.

HEAL THYSELF NATURAL LIVING COOK BOOK

Holiday Fruit Cake*

1 cup grated carrots
1 cup raisins
½ cup honey
¼ cup chopped dates
1 teaspoon cinnamon
1 teaspoon allspice
½ teaspoon nutmeg

¼ teaspoon ground
  cloves
1¾ cups water
1½ cups whole wheat
  flour
1 teaspoon. baking soda
½ cup bran

Cook the carrots, raisins, dates, honey and spices in the water for 10 minutes. Cool.
Mix together the flour, baking soda and bran.
Add to the carrot mixture.
Mix together well.
 Pour into non-stick loaf pan or 9" x 9" baking dish.
Bake at 325° F for 45 minutes.

These recipes although very natural are a good example of a "natural alternative," but are poor food combinations. They should not be eaten by anyone beyond the sophomore level and rarely by anyone else.

Desserts   117

Whipped Tofu Creme Topping

14 ounces package soft tofu
5 tablespoons soy milk (plain or vanilla)
5 tablespoons maple syrup
1 tablespoon Lemon juice
2 teaspoons vanilla extract

Purée all ingredients in a blender until very smooth. Chill at least two hours before serving.

Carob Sauce

1 cup water
2 teaspoons vanilla
2 tablespoons honey or natural liquid sweetener
2 tablespoons arrowroot powder or cornstarch
2 tablespoons roasted carob powder

½ teaspoon powdered coffee substitute (optional)

Combine all ingredients.

Bring to a boil, stirring constantly.

Remove from heat when thickened.

Makes 1¼ cups.

Fruit Squares

1 cup raisins
1 cup mixed dried fruit
½ cup almonds
2 tablespoons wheat germ
¼ cup sunflower seeds, ground in blender
¼ cup orange juice

Chop raisins, dried fruit and almonds.
Combine with wheat germ, ground sunflower seeds, and enough juice to moisten.
Press into an 8" baking pan lined with wax paper.
Cover and let harden in the refrigerator for several hours.
To serve, cut into squares with a knife dipped in hot water.

Makes 8 1" candies

Frozen Banana Creme*

4 large frozen bananas
1 teaspoon peanut butter

Cut bananas into chunks, and place in food processor fitted with steel blade.
Pulse until chopped.
Add peanut butter and process until bananas are smooth and creamy.
Serve immediately

This recipe although very natural, is a good example of a "natural alternative" but a poor food combination. It should not be eaten by anyone beyond the sophomore level and rarely by anyone else.

Homemade Applesauce

6 large apples
1 tablespoon Lemon juice
2 tablespoons water

½ teaspoon cinnamon
maple syrup to taste (optional)

Peel, core, and cut up apples.
Place them in a saucepan with lemon juice and water.
Cover and cook about 20 minutes, or until apples are very soft.
Stir in cinnamon and maple syrup, and blend until smooth.

Frozen Fruit Sorbet

1 cup pineapple juice
1 frozen banana, sliced

½ - 1 cup frozen or fresh blueberries or strawberries, sliced

2 cups frozen pineapple, sliced

Blend juice in blender at medium speed.
While blender is running, add slices of frozen fruit through the feed opening in the blender lid.
Blend mixture until it has a "soft serve" consistency.
Pour into serving dishes.
Serve immediately or store in freezer for a short time before serving.

Serves 6

Fruit Compote

½ cup dried apricots (about 4 - 6 ounces)

½ cup dried figs

½ cup raisins

3 cups apple juice or cider

1 teaspoon vanilla

1 orange, juiced

pinch of cinnamon, coriander, cardamon, ginger, and nutmeg

Rinse the dried fruit in a strainer.

Place in a sauce pot.

Cover with the juice and bring to a boil, simmering for 30 minutes or longer until the fruit has swelled and is soft.

Add the spices, vanilla and orange juice.

Simmer for 5 to 10 minutes longer.

The fruit should be plump, with a little liquid left in the pan.

Live Food Variation: Combine raw ingredients in a blender or food processor. Process until smooth.

Carob Tofu Pie*

Crust:

1 cup lightly roasted almonds

¼ cup unsweetened, finely ground carob powder
1 teaspoon vanilla extract:

⅛ teaspoon almond extract
1 tablespoon Liquid lecithin:
1 tablespoon maple syrup

Filling:

2¼ pounds firm tofu

¾ cup unsweetened, finely ground carob powder

2½ teaspoons vanilla extract

¾ teaspoon almond extract

¾ cup maple syrup

⅔ cup cold water
2 teaspoons powdered agar
Whipped soy cream (for garnish)

To make crust: Preheat oven to 375° F.

With metal blade in place, add almonds to the work bowl of food processor.

Pulse on and off until chopped medium-fine.
Add carob powder, vanilla extract, almond extract, lecithin and maple syrup. Process only until well mixed. Press into bottom (not sides) of a well greased 9½" spring form pan and bake for 8 minutes.
Allow to cool completely before filling.

Heal Thyself Natural Living Cook Book

To make filling: Squeeze most of the moisture out of the tofu.

Add to food processor.

Process until smooth and creamy.

Add carob powder, vanilla and almond extracts. Process until well mixed. In a small saucepan, combine maple syrup and water. Mix well.

Sprinkle agar over the top. Let stand one minute to soften. bring to a boil, then reduce heat and continue boiling for 30 seconds.

Cool for about 5 minutes.

With machine running, slowly pour agar liquid into the tofu-carob mixture.

Process a few seconds more to mix well.

Pour on top of the crust and chill for 15 - 20 minutes.

Variations: To filling add either peaches, apricots, or banana; reduce or eliminate carob powder, depending on your tastes. To Crust: Substitute raw cashews for almonds.

*THIS IS FOR THAT VERY SPECIAL OCCASION. BUT REMEMBER, IT IS STILL HEAVY AND Nor RECOMMENDED IF YOU RARELY EAT HEAVY FOODS.

Raspberry Tart Filling

2 cups apple raspberry juice

⅔ bar of agar-agar

Rinse agar-agar under running water for a few minutes until soft. It should have the texture of a wet sponge. Squeeze out excess liquid.

Tear agar into little pieces and add to the juice.

Bring juice and agar to a light boil; lower the flame, cover pan and simmer until agar is dissolved, about 5 - 7 minutes.

Pour mixture into shallow bowl.

Allow to cool, but not to set. Pour cooled filling into tart shell. Let filling set for 45 minutes to an hour in the refrigerator.

Lemon Custard Sauce

2 cups apple juice
3 tablespoons soy milk powder
1 lemon rind, grated
Juice from one lemon
3 tablespoons arrowroot powder (or)
2 tablespoons kuzu powder
1 teaspoon pure vanilla extract

Whisk together soy milk powder and juice.
Add lemon rind.
Bring to light boil.
Cover pan, lower flame and simmer for 6 - 7 minutes.
Dissolve arrowroot or kuzu powder in lemon juice.
Add to simmering liquid, stirring constantly until thick and custard like.
Pour into shallow bowl and let cool.
Serve over individual slices or raspberry tart.
For a hot dessert, serve warm.

Tofu Parfait

    2 cups soft tofu
    1 cup fresh or frozen blueberries
    2 small ripe bananas
    2 tablespoons maple syrup

    ½ teaspoon vanilla
    mint leaves for garnish

Blend all ingredients, except mint, and spoon into parfait or wine glasses.

Orange Custard Filling

2 cups apple juice
3 tablespoons soy milk powder
1 orange rind, grated
Juice from one lemon
3 tablespoons arrowroot powder (or)
2 tablespoons kuzu powder
1 teaspoon pure vanilla extract

This is the same as the recipe for lemon custard sauce (above), but an orange is used instead of a lemon for the grated rind and juice, and ½ bar of agar is added to the soy milk and apple juice, giving the custard a thicker consistency.

When adding agar, follow directions in raspberry filling recipe.

After you've let the orange custard cool, but not set, in a shallow bowl, pour it into a tart shell and allow to set for 45 minutes.

Almond Kanten Mousse

1 quart unsweetened apple juice
2 bars agar-agar torn into 1" pieces
1 tablespoon vanilla extract
1 tablespoon Lemon juice
6 tablespoons almond butter

½ cup plain soy milk

¼ cup slivered almonds, toasted
Fresh fruit

Combine the agar and apple juice in a large saucepan. Bring to a boil, then reduce to a simmer. Simmer, stirring until the agar is completely dissolved.

Pour into a large bowl or pan.

Refrigerate until the mixture is firm, about 1 hour.

Remove from refrigerator and purée in a blender, gradually adding the vanilla, lemon juice, almond butter and soy milk.

Purée until the kanten is smooth.

Return to refrigerator and chill at least an hour before serving

Garnish with fresh fruit — any kind of berries or peeled and sliced soft fruit such as peaches or nectarines add the toasted, slivered almonds.

Makes 6 servings.

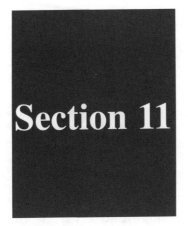

Section 11

Herbal "Folk" Recipes

Herbal "Folk" Recipes

THE USE OF HERBS AS A FOOD OR MEDICINE HAS BEEN USED by every religion and culture throughout human history. Herbs have had a variety of uses. Ancient cultures have used plants to heal the sick, protect against evil, flavor foods and adorn our bodies.

In Genesis 1:29 it is written:

> *And God said, Behold, I have given you every herb bearing seed, which is upon the face of all the earth, and every tree, in which is the fruit of a tree yielding seed, to you it shall be for meat.*

The use of herbs in our kitchens is a natural and time honored tradition. Many of us have memories of our mothers, aunts, or grandmothers fixing various teas for what "ails" us or for the annual "spring cleaning".

I have been blessed with the people I have met along my journey of life who have valued the uses of herbs. One such blessing was having the honor of being a student of Dr. John Moore, the self described "hobo doctor". Dr. Moore was a self made master herbalist. His knowledge of herbs, urban survival skills, spiritual survival and knowledge of the land was unparalleled. Despite his mastery, he was modest and shared his knowledge without thought to fame or fortune. This chapter is dedicated to his memory, lessons and wisdom.

Again I must remind you that the recipes in this chapter are "folk" recipes. There is no "scientific" evidence to support their effectiveness against any disease. They should not be used as a substitution of medicine and if you are on medication you should consult your physician first.

Since the effect of herbs is gentle, they must be taken daily over a period of time to be effective.

1 Single herbs and their "folk remedy" use

Herb	Uses
angelica	asthma, bronchitis
blueberry leaves	diabetes
bugleweed	cirrhosis of liver, asthma,
chamomile	stomach
chaparral	blood purifier, cancer
chuck weed	weight control, fever
club moss	liver malignancy
eyebright	eyes
fennel	appetite suppressant
ginger root-	motion sickness sore throat
goldenrod	fibroid tumors, kidney
lemongrass	hot weather, female problems
lily of valley	heart
linden flower	radiation sickness
lobelia	relaxant
lungwort	living disease
nettle	asthma
nutmeg	toxic liver, pancreas
oatstraw	increase memory
pansy	heart, high blood pressure

  HEAL THYSELF NATURAL LIVING COOK BOOK

Herb	Uses
parsley	high blood pressure
passion flower	persistent cough, anemia
peppermint	stomach
poke root	liver
red raspberry	arthritis, constipation
rosemary	headaches
shepherds purse	internal bleeding
strawberry leaves	eczema
thyme	thyroid problems
tarragon	stimulate appetite
uva uris	diabetes, kidney
wood betony	headaches, stress
yellow dock root	yellow jaundice
yerba santa	senility

II Herbal Tea Recipes

These recipes are not proven scientifically to cure any dis-eases. They are folk recipes. Do not substitute these recipes foe medicine, Consult your physician on use if you are taking any medication.

Senility
½ teaspoon periwinkle
½ teaspoon dandelion
½ teaspoon oatstraw

Detox Pancreas
Soak and boil shells of peanuts. Drink liquid.

Master Tea (I) for Women
1 ounce licorice root
1 ounce damiana
1 ounce hops

Master Tea (I) for Men
1 ounce nettles
1 ounce plantain leaves

Thyroid Tea
equal parts of each
comfrey
vervain
silverweed
marshmallow
nettle

Cancer

    1 ounce red clover
    1 ounce periwinkle
    1 ounce chaparral
    1 ounce Jamaican cramp bark

Cancer of uterus

    1 ounce weeping willow leaves
    1 ounce bark oat tree
    raw pumpkin seeds

Weight Reducing Tea

    1 ounce fennel
    1 ounce cornsilk
    1 ounce bedstraw
    1 ounce chick weed
    1 ounce prickle ash bark
    1 ounce uva ursi

Improve Memory

1 ounce of each

periwinkle	hawthorn berry
prickle ash bark	rosemary
	gota kola

Insomnia

1 ounce of each

hops	peppermint
licorice	valerian
lady's slipper	poke root

Male Tonic

1 ounce of each

sasprillia

orange peeling

gota kola

lemongrass

damiana

elder flower

hawthorn berries

ginseng

ginger root

Female Tonic

1 ounce of each

red raspberry leaves

gota kola

his hicus

orange peeling

damiana

blessed thistle

licorice root

cinnamon bark

orange blossom

dong quai

Sinus

1 ounce of each

saw palmetto

rose hip

mullein

golden seal

hops

red clover

Fasting Tea

1 ounce of each

spearmint

hops

chamomile

Fat Deposit Tea Blend

1 ounce of each

chickweed	mandrake
licorice root	papaya
saffron	hawthorn berries
gota kola	dandelion leaves
kelp	echinacea
black walnut leaves	bladderwrack

High blood Pressure

1 ounce of each

basswood leaves
peppergrass
nettle

III Herbal Ointments *

Skin ointment (infection of skin)

1 ounce chaparral
1 ounce comfrey root
1 ounce passion
add 1 pound of marigold flower for color (optional)

Constipation Tea

2 ounces senna leaves
rub on abdomen

Cough Rub

1 ounce each
patchouli, kelp, licorice root, ginger root, chamomile
use sunflower oil in preparing ointment

Tumor Ointment

1 ounce of each

St. John's worth   passion flower
Hawaiian sesame   make ointment, rub on
planters leaves   stomach

Pain Ointment

1 ounce each

jimsom weed
lavender

Cancer Ointment

1 ounce of each

white clover   violet leaves
red clover   beeswax
'pe' roxo   use corn oil
                 in preparation

Pain Ointment

equal amount of

oil of eucalyptus
camphor
wintergreen
peppermint

Burns

10 each of:

planters leaves   olive oil
comfrey   wheatgerm oil
almond

IV Preparation

Tea

Infusion:
Put fresh or dried herbs into a pot, and pour over boiling water. Let steep for at least 10 minutes.

Decoction: (Best for roots, bark or twip)

To extract active ingredients from roots.
Place chopped roots or bark in a saucepan with cold water.
Bring water to boil, simmer 15-20 minutes
     (reducing liquid by 2)
Strain. Use within 24 hours.

Ointment:

Use 1 pint oil for every 8 ounces of dried herbs.
     (use olive oil unless recipe calls for a different oil)
Place the herbs and oil in a glass bowl over a pot of simmering water.
Heat gently for three hours.
Strain through muslim cloth.
Pour oil in a dark sterile bottle
     (can store in cool, dark place for one year)
Take the infused oil, placed in a glass bowl .Place over a pot of boiling water. Add ½" square of beeswax and stir in liquid until wax is completely melted.
While still warm, pour into dark jars, let cool.
Adding the beeswax is optional.
The beeswax makes the ointment solid.
Any herbal tea can be made into an ointment.

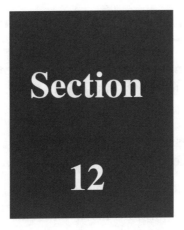

Section

12

Charts

Eating For Happiness*

Do Not Mix more than *four* foods, from more than two classifications, at any one meal.

Use *One Protein* food or *one starch* food per meal.

OIL slow digestion. Combines best fruit and green vegetables; combines poorly with starch and protein.

Tomato combines best with avocado and green vegetables.

Melon (all kinds) should always be eaten alone.

Avocado combines best with acid fruit, sprouts and vegetables. Use in moderation.

Wheatgrass should always be taken on an empty stomach. May mix carrot and green vegetable and sprout juices.

Seed Cheese goes well with ripe sub-acid fruit, banana, leafy greens, sprouts, or alone.

Use *Honey and Molasses* on an empty stomach to prevent fermentation.

Peanuts are high in protein, fat and starch and therefore difficult to digest.

Try eating one kind of FRUIT at a time or combining them according to type of seed:
stone fruit(peach, nectarine, apricot, cherry),
citrus fruit, core fruit (apples, pears) dried fruit,
melon fruit. Papaya goes well with all sub-acid fruit as well as banana.

Reprinted from *Survival into the 21st Century Natural Planetary Healers Manual:* by Viktoras Kulvinkas. pp. 267-69

HEAL THYSELF NATURAL LIVING COOK BOOK

What To Eat

☞ Organic live food is your medicare and your ticket to prolonged youth. Eat mostly natural food which appeal to you .

☞ Advance your diet according to the dictates of your body and the type of work you perform.

☞ Avoid all animal, processed, or cooked food, strong condiments and spices. Do not use the teeth to crush hard food. If it is hard to masticate, it shouldn't be b eaten.

☞ Grow your own food in your own garden: vegetables, fruits, sprouts, seven-day greens. Eventually eat fruit only.

When To Eat*

☞ Eat only when you are hungry and after the previous meal is digested.
Do not snacks between meals. Some people can have as much three or more meals in semi-digested, putrefactive state within the digestive tract.

☞ Eat the biggest meal at noon when sun activity is strongest. Solar vibrations aid digestion. Eat a small meal before sunset for a longer night after work.

☞ Never eat when in pain, emotionally upset, extremely tired or immediately after work.

Rest or relax for 45 minutes after a meal . For those with a delicate digestion, lie down for at least 10 minutes before a meal.

☞ Do not eat or drink after retiring for the night.

How To Eat*

☞ Begin with name of God. Be grateful, ask for control in appetite. Bring a tranquil mind to meals. Do not argue or rush.

☞ Enjoy the music of birds and brook, the silence of the sky. Enjoy your food.

☞ Do not drink (or eat) cold or hot (beyond 104° F) substances

☞ No liquid with meals. Drink at least thirty minutes before or three hours after a meal.

☞ Eat one food prior at a meal, or combine food correctly for best digestion. Eat juicy foods prior to concentration foods. Eat raw foods before cooked foods. Stop eating before you feel full.

Reprinted from   *Survival into the 21st Century Natural Planetary Healers Manual:* by Viktoras Kulvinkas. pp. 267-69

Chemistry of Food*

Acid Ash-: All grain (except millet), all meat, butter, cream, eggs, cheese, animal fats, sea foods, most nuts, dry peas, dry beans, most oils, lentils, peanuts, hulled sesame.

Mucus Inducing Foods-: All acid ash foods. All diary products. Sprouted grains, chick peas, lentils, seeds, nuts potato, yam. Slightly: Squash (Acorn, Butternut, Hubbard).

Alkaline Ash-: Most dried fruit, indoor greens, all grasses, dandelion, soybean sprouts, cucumber, almond, unhulled sesame, vegetables, olive oil, sprouts from most legumes.

Acid ph Fruit-: Current, grapefruit, kumquat, lemon, lime, loganberry, loquat, orange, pineapple, pomegranate, strawberry, tamarind, tangerine , tangelo, tomato. When ripe, all fruits produce alkaline effect in the bloodstream. Overacid condition can be generated in the stomach regions, affecting your whole body, from the intake of ascorbic acid (vitamin C), nicotinic acid, or any of the acidy vitamins, just as well as from eating unripe tomatoes, citrus or pineapple. Symptoms: dizziness, fainting, pressure on the eyes, headache, burning sensation in the stomach, bleeding of the gums.

Sub-Acid Fruit-: Apple, apricot, blackberry, cactus fruit, cherimoya, cherry, elderberry, gooseberry, grape, guava, huckleberry, jujube, mango, nectarine, papaya, papaw, peach, pear, persimmon, plum, kiwi, raspberry, sapodilla, sapote.

Melon-: banana, cantaloupe, casaba, christmas, crenshaw, honeydew, watermelon.

Acid Fruit-: Most berries pineapple and pomegranate leave the bloodstream more acid. When badly combined, or eaten in large quantity most food can leave the body more acid.

Alkaline Fruit-: Citrus, tomatoes, most sweet fruit and those fruit listed sub-acid column leave the body more alkaline. Unripe, depleted soil sub-acid fruit are really acid.

Soaked Dried Fruit-: such as figs, apples, apricot, peaches, dates and pears leave the body more alkaline. However, too much or too frequent or badly combined can caused fermentation and acidity in the bloodstream.

Colored Vegetables-: Beets, carrots, red cabbage, cauliflower, corn, eggplant, parsnip, rutabaga, squashes, turnips, slightly mucus including.

Cooked Vegetables-: During transition to raw foods all starchy food can be cooked. Eventually, lightly steam or baked the vegetables listed can be cooked. Eventually, lightly steamed or baked the vegetables listed as fruit, green or colored. To slow down a rapid cleansing reaction slightly cooked vegetables may be the used. Under such circumstances, you might want to blend together some raw and some cooked vegetables.

Reprinted from   *Survival into the 21st Century Natural Planetary Healers Manual:* by Viktoras Kulvinkas. pp. 267-69

Natural Vitamin Supplements *

Calcium Forms   oatstraw & comfrey herbs, sprouts, carrots, green leafy vegetables, nut milk, soy milk

Vitamin A/D   carrots

Vitamin B   yeast, bee pollen

Vitamin C   rosehips herb tea

Vitamin E   alfalfa, wheatgrass

Minerals   kelp, other sea plants, spirula, blue/green manna

Fun Foods   freshly prepared popcorn, brown rice cakes, dried fruits, (banana chips, pineapple, apricots, raisins), banana custard, frozen fruit juice, (instead of ice cubes), chilled fruit (grapes, oranges, baked apples).

Reprinted from   *Heal Thyself for Health and Longevity*
Queen Afua, A&B Publishers Group

Natural Living Cycles: 1

REJUVENATION		HARMONY IN BODY,
+	=	MIND & SPIRIT
PURIFICATION		

Rejuvenation = Vegetables (live and steamed) Chlorophyll, wheatgrass and Spirulina Rejuvenating herbs fruits.

Purification = Enemas, herbal laxatives and colonics Purification herbs.

Levels of Mastery

1 *Freshman* Organic chicken and fish (unshelled fish) baked or broiled. 75 % steamed vegetables, 25 % raw vegetables. Whole grain, such as brown rich and bulgar wheat.

2 *Sophomore*-Soya meats, beans, peas, nuts, seeds and sprouts. 50 % steamed vegetables, 50 % raw vegetables. Whole grains, such as brown rice and bulgar wheat.

3 *Junior* Sprouts (alfalfa, mung and others). 25 % steamed vegetables, 75 % raw vegetables. Light grains, such as tabouli and couscous.

4 *Senior* Live uncooked foods and sprouted proteins. 100 % raw diet of fresh fruits, vegetables, juices, nuts and seeds (pre-cooked, eaten in moderation)

5 *Master*- 50% of diet consists of juices and herb teas. 50 % of diet consists of fresh fruits and vegetables. No grains, nuts or seeds.

6 *Ph.D.*- A "Ph.D." purified would consists of 100% pure air and water. Alas, we must first cleanse the planet.

FOOD COMBINING FOR EASIER DIGESTION

PROTEIN - Meat, eggs, fish, (not recommended) nuts (Most) fermented seed sauce, soybeans, cooked or sprouted seed: sunflower, sesame, pumpkin, chia.

P O O R

STARCHES - Grains cooked or sprouted, mature beans and peas, peanuts, potatoes, butternut, chick peas, cooked or sprouted, winter squash: acorn, hubbard.

GOOD   VEGETABLES   GOOD

POOR To FAIR

Buckwheat lettuce
Leafy Greens
Radish Greens
Sunflower Greens
Watercress
Weed
Asparagus
Beet
Carrot (Mildly Starchy)

Fresh Peas
Jersalem Artichoke
Parsnip (Mildly Starchy)
Green Peas
Sweet Pepper
Summer Squash
Turnip
Celery

POOR

Sprouts: Mung, lentil, alfalfa, fenugreek, radish, cucumber (Eat only with other vegetables)

POOR   POOR   POOR

ACID FRUIT
Grapefruit
Lemon
Lime
Orange
Strawberry
Pineapples
Pomegranate
Plums (Prunes)
Blackberries
Tangerines
Tanberries
Raspberries
Kumguat
Ugli

SUB-ACID FRUIT
Apple
Apricot,
Kiwi
Fresh Flag
Grape
Mango
Papaya
Pear
Peach
Sweet Cherry
Blueberries
Nectarines

SWEET FRUIT
Banana
Date
Dried Flag
Dried Fruit
Raisin
Persimon

GOOD COMBINATION
Protein and leafy Greens
starch and vegetables
Oil and acid subacid
FRUIT
Oil and leafy greens

POOR COMBINATION
Protein and acid fruit
Leafy Greens and acid
Fruit Leafy Greens and
subacid Fruit

BAD COMBINATION
Protein and starch
Oil and starch
Fruit and starch

149

Vegetarian Substitute
Dairy and egg substitutes

Milk-   soy milk, nut milk, rice or oat milk, banana milk

Yogurt-   soy yogurt

Cheese-   mashed soft tofu small amounts of misco or tamari to add saltiness

Butter-   soy margarine, vegetable oil (d cup oil for 1 cup butter), nut butters, fruit butters or preserves to spread on bread

Sour Cream-   blend soft tofu with lemon juice and herbs

Eggs
To replace 1 egg in baked goods:
1 teaspoon commercial egg replacer, plus 2 tablespoons water;
1 tablespoons arrowroot,
1 tablespoon soyflour, plus 2 tablespoons water;
2 tablespoons flour
½ tablespoons vegetable shortening,
½ tablespoons baking powder, plus 2 tablespoons water;
⅛ pound tofu blended with the liquid in the recipe you are using; large banana, mashed

To replace eggs in casseroles, burgers and loaves- mashed avocado, tahini and nut butter, or rolled oats.

Sweet Substitute

These measurements are substitutions for 1 cup of sugar.

Natural Sweetener	Substitute	Liquid Reduction
Honey	¾ cup	⅛ cup
Maple Syrup	¾ cup	⅙
Maple Granules	1 cup	
Molasses	½ cup	-
Date Sugar	1 cup	-
Barley Malt	1½ cup	slightly
Fruit Juice Concentrate	1½ cup	⅛ cup

Food Alternative

Low Vibration Foods	High Vibration Foods
	(Eat between Noon & 4 p.m. only)
cheese	rennetless unsalted cheese or grated tofu.
chocolate	carob
cereals (commercial)	whole wheat oats, granola
corn starch	arrow root powder
cow's milk	soy milk, nut milk, goats milk, kafir, mother's milk
dannon yogurt	browncow yogurt *(best not to eat!)*
eggs	organic eggs *(try to avoid)*
fruit juice (bottled/canned)	fresh squeezed/pressed fruit juice
gelatin	agar-agar
grains (other)	millet, couscous, bulgar
grits	soy grits, barley grits
ice cream	soy ice cream
margarine	soya margarine
oil	cold pressed olive oil
pancakes	buckwheat, whole wheat, bran or flax seed pancakes
peanut butter	fresh unsweetened peanut butter
salt	sea salt, kelp, dulse
vinegar	apple cider vinegar
water	distilled or spring water
white bread	whole wheat
white flour	whole wheat flour or barley
white macaroni	whole wheat macaroni
white rice	brown rice
white sugar	raw honey, maple syrup, black strap molasses, fructose

Note   *If you have a high percentage of live food in your diet or are beyond the sophomore level in Queen Afua's natural living program many of the heavier recipes which contain tofu, nuts, rice, gravies or pasta may be too heavy and should not be eaten.*

HEAL THYSELF NATURAL LIVING COOK BOOK

About the Author

Diane Ciccone has been on the path of purification for over twenty five years. She believes in the purification of the body temple through the art of fasting and the natural living process. She has studied with John E. Moore, the Reverend Philip Valentine and Queen Afua.

Diane is a graduate of Colgate University and Hofstra School of Law. She is in private practice in New York City. She lives in New Jersey with her husband and daughter and when she is not working or studying, she can be found in her kitchen cooking new and healthy recipes for her family.

People often ask me why did I chose to become a vegetarian. I tell the story my father told me, that a s a little girl I would sit at the dinner table, sometimes till bedtime, because I kept chewing the meat and didn't want to swallow. As a teenager, I read Adele Davis's Eat Right to Live, Upton Sinclair's Slaughterhouse and the Autobiography of Malcolm X. These three books gave me th resolve and the commitment to act out my belief that eating meat was unnecessary and detrimental for good health. In 1970 it wasn't fashionable or acceptable to be a vegetarian. I was ill prepared for the daily challenges to learn how to eat differently than those around me. This book is important to me because it gives you simple recipes to ensure a good wholesome diet.

In closing. I hope this book will be a guide in your quest for a healthier and lighter diet. As you make this journey remember that old adage, *you eat what you are and are what you eat.*

Index

Acorn, 68, 83, 145, 149
Agar, 122-124, 127-128
Agar-agar, 56, 124, 128, 152
Alfalfa, 40, 47, 55, 59, 147-149
Allspice, 29, 75, 82, 114, 117
Almond, 51, 115, 122-123, 128, 138, 145
Almond Cookies, 115
Almond Kanten Mousse, 128
Almonds, 27-28, 115, 119, 122-123, 128
Alzheimer, 7
Apple Ginger Marinade, 76
Apple Whiz, 32
Argula, 54, 56
Arrowroot, 97, 118, 125, 127, 150
Art, 153
Arthritis, 133
Artichoke, 95, 149
Artichokes, 40, 95
Arugula, 47, 54
Asparagus, 48, 149
Asparagus Ginger Salad, 48
Asthma, 132
Avocado, 22, 88, 109-110, 142, 150
Avocado Supreme, 88
Avocados, 109

Baby Zucchini Salad, 47
Baked Macaroni & Cheese, 98
Balsamic, 47, 50, 54
Bamboo, 103
Banana, 28, 30, 119-120, 123, 142, 145, 147, 149-150
Banana Smoothie 28
Bananas, 28, 119, 126
Bean Sprout and Watercress, 50
Bed, 56, 58-59, 88-89, 108-109
Bedstraw, 135
Black-eyed Pea Salad, 57
Blackberries, 149
Bladderwrack, 137
Blessed, 130, 136

Blood Sugar Tonic, 40
Blueberries, 116, 120, 126, 149
Breakfast Rice Pudding, 14
Broccoli, 18, 55, 68, 89, 97, 100

Calcium, 147
Carob Sauce, 118
Carob Tofu Pie, 122
Carrot Ginger Zing, 39
Carrot Pate, 20
Carrot Salad, 51
Carrot Soup, 69
Carrot & Cabbage, 40
Carrot & Spinach, 41
Carrot & String Bean, 41
Carrot & Turnip, 40
Cauliflower Couscous Pate, 21
Cauliflower Pilaf, 89
Cauliflower & Argula Salad, 54
Chemistry of Food, 145
Citrus Wake-Up, 42
Coconut Milk, 27
Coconut-Almond Milk, 28
Comfrey, 28, 134, 137-138, 147
Comfrey Pineapple Cooler, 28
Couscous Salad, 48
Cranapple, 43
Cranberries, 43
Cream of Navy Bean Soup, 65
Creamy Tofu Dip with Garlic & Dill, 74
Crunchy Granola, 15
Cucumber Cooler, 39
Cucumbers, 107
Curried Tofu, 102
Curry Mixed Vegetables, 74

Damiana, 134, 136
Dandelion Greens, 84
Decoction, 139
Dillweed, 73

Eating for Happiness, 142
Echinacea, 137
Eczema, 133
Eggless Soy Mayonnaise, 60
Eggplant Salad, 52
Elderberry, 145
Eucalyptus, 138
Eyebright, 132

Fenugreek, 149
Food Combining for easier Digestion, 152
Food Alternatives, 152
French Toast, 13
Frozen Banana Creme, 119
Frozen Fruit Sorbet, 120
Fruit 'n' Flax, 30
Fruit Compote, 121
Fruit Squares, 119

Ginger Ale, 33
Ginger Cookies, 114
Gingery Tahini Sauce, 74
Grape Spritzer, 30
Grapefruit & Orange, 43
Green Drink, 41
Grilled Corn on the Cob, 93
Guacamole, 109
Gumbo Salad, 56
Goldenrod, 132
Gooseberry, 145
Grapes, 30, 147
Guacamole, 109
Guava, 145

Herb Vinegar, 60
Herbal Tea Recipes, 134
Hobo, 130
Hoisin Sauce, 66
Holiday Fruit Cake, 117
Homemade Applesauce, 76
Homemade Teriyaki Sauce, 76
Hot Carob Drink, 35

Hot Spiced Cider, 29
How To Eat, 144
Humus, 109

Kale (Steamed), 85
Kiwi, 145, 149
Kumguat, 149
Kumquat, 145

Lemon Custard Sauce, 125
Lemon Garlic Dressing, 61

Mango Strawberry Salad, 56
Maple Soy Frosting, 116
Marinated Broccoli & Cauliflower, 89
Marinated Mushrooms, 19
Melon Orange Frappe, 29
Mint Cooler, 31
Miso Dressing, 61
Muesli, 15
Mushroom Spinach Salad, 57
Mustard, 77
Mustard Marinade, 75

Natural Living Cycles, 148
Natural Vitamin Supplements, 147
Nectarines, 128, 149
No Bake Blueberry Couscous Cake, 116
Noodles with Sesame Ginger Sauce, 99
Nut & Seed Milk, 27
Nutmeg, 14, 21, 69, 83, 104, 114, 117, 121, 132

Oatstraw, 132, 134, 147
Orange Custard Filling, 127
Orange Mist, 31
Oranges, 29, 34, 42, 147

Pansy, 132
Paprika, 52, 55, 66, 98

Pasta & Broccoli, 100
Peach & Strawberry, 43
Pineapple Supreme, 42
Pineapple Supreme Plus, 42
Pocket Fillers, 107
Potato Leek Soup, 70
Prebreakfast Drink, 13

Raspberry Tart Filling, 124
Raspberries, 149
Ratatouille, 87
Relish Salad, 59
Rice Mushroom Casserole, 94
Rice Milk, 27
Root Beer, 34
Root Salad, 58
Rosehips, 147

Safflower, 22, 60-61, 65, 74, 86
Saffron, 95, 137
Savory Daikon, 88
Scrambled Tofu, 14
Seaweed Gumbo, 90
Seaweed Vegetable Soup, 68
Sesame Garlic Dressing, 62
Sesame Sauce, 73
Sesame Spread, 108
Sesame String Beans, 92
So You Said You Wanted A Salad,
   47
Soy Mayonnaise, 78
Spicy pasta Salad, 50
Spirulina Sauce, 78
Split Pea Soup, 66
Spring Sweep, 39
Sprout Salad, 59
Stuffed Celery Sticks, 22
Stuffed Endive Leaves, 22
Stuffed Squash, 83
Sun Tea Cocktails, 32
Sushi Roll ups, 110
Sweet & Tangy Marinade, 75
Sweet 'n' Sour Noodles, 97

Sweet Substitutes, 151

Tahini Cookies, 106
Tea & Fruit Pop, 32
Tempeh Jambalaya, 104
Tofu & Cherry Tomato Kebobs, 103
Tofu Cottage Cheese, 73
Tofu Creole, 82
Tofy Eggless Salad, 58
Tofu Loaf, 101
Tofu Mexican Style, 101
Tofu Parfait, 126
Tofu Sour Cream, 77
Tofu Spread, 108
Tofu Stuffed Peppers, 91
Tofu with Ginger & Onion, 102
Tropical Fruit Tea, 34
Turnip Greens, 86
Two Bean Salad with Fresh herbs,
   53

Ugli, 149

Vegetable Broth, 65
Vegetable Pulao Rice, 96
Vegetable Salad, 55
Vegetable Stew, 67
Vegetarian Substitutions, 151
Vegetarian Paella, 95
Veggie Cocktail, 39
Veggie Pocket, 107

Watercress, 22-23, 28, 41, 47, 50, 149
Watermelon , 43
What To Eat, 143
When To Eat, 143
Wheatgrass, 142, 147-148
Whipped Tofu Creme Topping, 118

Zucchini Soup, 69